D1213103

Complete Postcards
from the
Americas

Blaise Cendrars

Complete Postcards from the Americas

Poems of Road and Sea

DOCUMENTAIRES

DOCUMENTARIES

FEUILLES DE ROUTE

OCEAN LETTERS

SUD-AMÉRICAINES

SOUTH AMERICAN WOMEN

Translated, with an Introduction, by
Monique Chefdor

UNIVERSITY OF CALIFORNIA PRESS
BERKELEY ● LOS ANGELES ● LONDON
1976

University of California Press
Berkeley and Los Angeles, California

University of California Press, Ltd.
London, England

Copyright © 1976 by The Regents of the University of California

The French Text of Cendrars's poems © Editions Denoël 1957 forms
part of *Du monde entier au coeur du monde,* the Denoël edition of
the complete poems of Blaise Cendrars

Library of Congress Catalog Card Number: 73-94445
ISBN: 0-520-02716-7

Printed in the United States of America

CONTENTS

ACKNOWLEDGMENTS

I wish to thank the Éditions Denoël for permission to reproduce and translate the poems of Blaise Cendrars presented in this volume. Éditions Denoël, with Myriam Cendrars for *Inédits Secrets*, also holds the copyright for the material from Blaise Cendrars's complete works quoted in the introduction.

I am greatly indebted to Henry Miller for permission to consult Blaise Cendrars's correspondence in the collection he donated to the Research Library, University of California, Los Angeles, and for permission to quote a passage from his article on Cendrars, "Salute from Afar," at the beginning of my introduction; to Brooke Whiting, curator of rare books in the Department of Special Collections, University of California, Los Angeles, for his expert and kind assistance in my research; and to the Manuscripts Department of the University of Virginia Library, Charlottesville, for permission to consult Dos Passos's special collection.

I wish to express particular gratitude to Raymone Cendrars-Sauser for her illuminating and sensitive response to my queries concerning the creative and personal texture of her husband's life, and for giving me her permission to consult manuscripts and correspondence of Blaise Cendrars in the Jacques Doucet reserve library, and to Angèle Lévesque, widow of the late critic and Blaise Cendrars's lifelong friend, Jacques-Henry Lévesque, for kindly offering photographs from her collection as illustrations for this volume, and especially for her warm encouragement and for generously sharing with me knowledgeable insights and her store of invaluable information.

A summer grant from Scripps College made possible the preliminary research.

M. C.

Scripps College
Claremont, California

INTRODUCTION

*To reassemble the multitudinous and contradictory
elements which constitute the essential character of
our time, to body it forth in prose and verse as tough
elastic vital and spontaneous as the raw plasma of life
itself, this has been the task done on the side as it
were. Reams and reams of words tossed off, you might
say, by a Titan who by way of recreation ceased his
endless rampages to take up the pen now and then.*
—*Henry Miller*[1]

Thus did Henry Miller "salute" Blaise Cendrars "from
afar" in 1960, summing up in these forceful and sugges-
tive words the titanic achievement of the Swiss-born poet
of the entire world, whom he had recognized, as early as
1938, as the "most contemporary of contemporaries."[2]

Indeed, Blaise Cendrars, the "Great adventurer known
the world over," the "Marco Polo of the twentieth cen-
tury,"[3] "The Homer of the Transsiberian,"[4] may be
viewed as the embodiment of our time, the epitome of the
century. He is probably the first writer attuned to the
transplanetary sensitivity of the future, but he is also the
last bard of the roamers of the road and the sea, the
representative of a gradually disappearing race of free-
wheeling individualistic wanderers. A forerunner of the
Dada state of mind and among the first on the cubist
front, he spent his life staking out new territory and left a

body of work so far ahead of his time that Ferreira de Castro sees it as "solitary, like one of those distant islands of which he likes to speak and where no one before him ever landed."[5]

Yet another image comes to mind, for Cendrars's solitary figure was a world-encompassing one. If he ever felt like a "squirrel whirling in the cage of the meridians,"[6] he also knew how to crack the bounds and escape into the freest of lives, where he would weave the web of his multifaceted vision into a work throbbing with the rhythm of the universe.

For Cendrars, living was an act of magic, as he repeated time and again in his numerous works. The facts of his life are wrapped up in the clouds of a legend to which he himself contributed as much as his biographers, not because he cared to mystify the reader but because the biography of the mind was as real to him as the data of daily life. Now that most of the facts have been unraveled from fiction, reality hardly falls short of the legend.

FROM FREDDY SAUSER TO BLAISE CENDRARS: THE GENESIS OF A POET, 1887-1912

Blaise Cendrars, who chose to be born in a hotel at 216, rue Saint-Jacques in Paris, was actually Frédéric Sauser born in La Chaux-de-Fonds in Switzerland on September 1, 1887. The Sauser family was part of the Anabaptist group of Bôle (French Jura) which had fled to Sigriswil, a mountain farmers' village in the Bern district; this fact proved the tradition of rebellion in his heritage, said Cendrars in a record issued in 1957 by Radio Suisse Romande entitled "Paroles de Romandie." Cendrars's father, Georges Frédéric Sauser, was described by Cendrars in Vol à Voile as a fanciful impractical inventor and his mother, Marie Louise Dorner of Kusnacht in the district of Zurich, as a dreamy hypersensitive woman. Two

entries in the municipal registry of La Chaux-de-Fonds
list Georges Frédéric Sauser as a merchant in the clock
trade. But if perhaps not an inventor, Cendrars's father
was undoubtedly a versatile and enterprising individual
who took his family along through the ups and downs of a
series of business ventures across Europe and Egypt. Cen-
drars's early childhood was thus stamped with the char-
acter of his future restlessness. There is evidence of some
schooling in a German gymnasium and at the interna-
tional school in Naples, but most of the boy's education
must have come from the books he used to borrow or
steal from his father until the Sausers settled in Neu-
châtel and placed their younger son Freddy in a business
school. This vocational training was so little suited to the
future poet that he spent more time sailing on the lake
than in class and was soon to run away. At least so
Cendrars tells us in *Vol à Voile*, the story of his famous
escape from the second-floor window of his parents'
house, according to which he went to the railroad station,
where he caught the first train to come in, and through
Basel, Berlin and Munich started on the odyssey he
immortalized in *La Prose du Transsibérien et de la Petite
Jeanne de France*:

> And, me too, I left to accompany the jewelry dealer who
>   was going to Harbin
> . . . .
> I slept on the trunks and I was thrilled to be able to
>   play with the nickel-plated Browning he had also
>   given me

Thus Freddy would have traveled with a jewelry dealer,
the legendary Rogovine he had met in Munich, who, as
the legend goes, took him on as an assistant in his
international smuggling and commercial deals in Russia,
Siberia, and China. Truth has evidently been turned into
fantasy, but the seventeen-year-old youth did in fact
spend several momentous years in prerevolutionary

Russia. It has been established by Jean-Claude Lovey and
Jean Buhler and confirmed by the notebooks and corre-
spondence recently published in *Inédits Secrets* by his
daughter Myriam Cendrars that he worked for three years
(1904-1907) as a Franco-German correspondent for a
watchmaker named Leuba who lived at 34 Gorokhovy
Street in Saint Petersburg. The long lists of books he
borrowed from the Saint Petersburg library reveal the
variety of his intellectual interests, and a manuscript
entitled "Alea" shows that his literary endeavors date
back to that first Russian experience. "Alea" later became
Moganni Nameh. It is probable that in that period he also
composed *Novgorod, la légende de l'or gris et du silence*,
listed in the Talvart and J. Place bibliography as published
in Moscow in 1909 by Sozonoff in a translation by R. R.
Although Cendrars consistently placed *Novgorod* at the
head of all his bibliographies, no trace of it has been
found.

In April 1907 Freddy Sauser returned to Switzerland,
going first to Basel and then to Neuchâtel. There he
stayed until September, according to his correspondence
with Hélène, a girl from Saint Petersburg. At the thresh-
old of what had already become an eventful life, the
accidental death of Hélène seems to have brought him to
the edge of despair, for the diary of that period ends
abruptly on a cry of anguish: "I spit on life that does not
listen to life."[7]

In the following years legend and fact are again inter-
twined. Most biographers of Cendrars record that he
settled in Multien, a Paris suburb where he kept bees and
cultivated medicinal plants to earn his living. This informa-
tion is substantiated, however, only by Cendrars's own
account in several short stories. It would be the moment
when he met Gustave Lerouge, the writer of popular
horror stories whom Cendrars often acknowledged as the
most accomplished craftsman of words. It has also been

said that in 1908 Cendrars was a juggler in a London music hall, sharing a room with a clown called Charlie Chaplin, a fact denounced by T'sertevens as pure fiction and questioned by most other biographers.

Cendrars's correspondence with his brother reveals that in 1909 he was in Bern, studying medicine and philosophy at the university. This is where he met Fela Poznanska, who later became his first wife. Wanderlust, however, had taken a firm hold on him, and he soon took off for Belgium. In April 1910 he wrote from Brussels to a friend in Austria that he was earning his living as a comedian. At the same time he continued to pursue his literary interests, and at La Panne, on the North Sea, he wrote an article on Rémy de Gourmont, whom he greatly admired and whose influence on him he always recognized, even much later in his life.[8]

After leaving Belgium Cendrars went to Paris where he settled at the famous 216, rue Saint-Jacques. The solitary year of intensive reading he spent there must have been spiritually decisive, for he mythopoetically chose the hotel at that address as his birthplace. In Paris he wrote a tale entitled "Conte," which remained unpublished until *Inédits Secrets* came out, and translated *La Messe des Morts* by Stanislaw Przybyszewski. He had not yet penetrated the writers' and artists' circles of Paris, but he did make the acquaintance of the Swiss sculptor August Suter who in the years immediately following, became a reliable and helpful friend.

The time had not yet come for him to be born to the literary world; Frédéric Sauser was not yet Blaise Cendrars. The rumble of trans-European trains and the storms of the high seas would claim him first.

He returned to Saint Petersburg in April 1911 and spent some time in Streilna, by the Gulf of Finland. The letters he wrote then to August Suter reveal his growing awareness of his vocation as a writer. He expresses eagerness to come back to Paris as soon as he has enough money. But his return to France was to be via the United States; providentially, in October 1911, Fela sent him a steamship ticket to New York. He embarked in Libau, Latvia, on the SS *Birma* on November 21 and landed in New York on December 12, 1911.

The diary Cendrars kept during the train trip from Russia to Varsovia and Libau, as well as throughout the crossing is a moving and enlightening document on the genesis of the writer, his struggle with and his gradual control over his buoyant, divided, hypersensitive nature. Until then he had appeared as a romantic, introspective, exacerbated young man who felt he had already lived all that destiny held for him and who was still strongly influenced by his wide and varied reading. As soon as he boarded the *Birma* he plunged into the quick of reality with the lucidity and synesthetic sensitivity to his environment which would characterize his future writings. When a violent storm broke at sea during his voyage, there is for a few pages in the diary a sudden rupture of style into a vibrant, terse, original vigor of imagery that foreshadowed the poetic revolution he was to bring about a year later. Frédéric Sauser was not only sailing to New York, to a new land and to a woman he loved, but he had embarked on the voyage of his destiny as a writer.

As deeply reserved personally as he was prolific as a storyteller, Cendrars never enlarged on his New York experience in his writings. Only the recently released diaries indicate the decisive turn in his inner life these months meant. It is probably characteristic that the first appearance of his new signature, Blaise Cendrart, changed a year later to Cendrars, dates from December 18, 1911, a few days after his arrival in New York. Later he assumed a detached tone of mockery when he provided an explanation for the choice of name in *Une nuit dans la forêt*. Telling of a friend who pretended to have found the source of his name in lines from Nietzsche,

Und alles wird mir nur zur Asche
Was ich liebe, was ich fasse,

[All I love and embrace
To ashes is soon reduced]

he added laughingly that "Blaise" was a phonetic trans-
mutation of *braise* ("embers").[9] As *cendres* means
"ashes," the significance of his choice is clear. It could
not be pure whimsical fantasy on his part since through-
out his life Cendrars insisted that "to write is to burn
alive."[10] Undoubtedly the fire was starting to consume
him.

In New York he lived in a number of places (Brooklyn,
West 67th Street, West 96th Street, among others), some-
times with Fela and sometimes away from her. He tried
hopelessly to latch on to any number of jobs, but he spent
most of his time reading in the New York Public Library
and roaming the streets after the library closed. A series of
dynamic, witty, and perceptive sketches of people he met
hold the seeds of many poems translated in this volume.
On the other hand, Cendrars's letters to Fela and to Suter
show him increasingly tortured by the contradictions of
his being, torn between the demands of life and those of
his creative urge. This antinomy, which he was never
able to resolve, was already so overwhelming that he felt
the need to dramatize it in an immature but psycho-
logically revealing play, "Danse macabre de l'amour," the
modernized Chatterton-like struggle of an artist shackled
by his environment in a network of fetters, including
those of love.

It is difficult to believe that this play, which remained
unpublished until *Inédits Secrets* appeared,[11] falls rough-
ly into the same period as the poem *Les Pâques à New
York*, which was written on Easter night in April 1911.
Cendrars himself recalled the event in radio interviews.[12]

Roaming endlessly through the city streets from Brook-
lyn to his lodgings uptown, he stopped in Saint Bar-
tholomew's Church where an oratorio by Haydn was
being played. He left the church before the end of the
performance, walked home, went to bed, starved and
exhausted, woke up in the middle of the night and wrote
the poem. By itself, *Pâques à New York* ranks Cendrars
with Villon, Baudelaire, Whitman, the Crane of "The
Bridge," Eliot, and Auden. After this poetic trance he had
but one idea in mind—to return to Paris—and he did so a
few weeks later.

FROM THE CUBIST FRONT TO THE
FOREIGN LEGION, 1912-1915

After a short visit in Geneva, Frédéric Sauser, from now
on definitely Blaise Cendrars, penniless and unknown,
arrived in Paris with *Les Pâques* in his pocket. There, in
pre-Dada cubist Paris, the twenty-five-year-old poet, full
of the "new life" and the "universal lyricism" throbbing
all over the earth, the new regime of human personality
being shaped by the accelerated mechanical beat of the
"prodigious centers of industrial activities"[13]—New
York, Berlin, Moscow—found his natural habitat.

Paris was then the crucible of all the new isms in poetry
and art which were to spread all over Europe: unanimism,
suprematism, vorticism, constructivism, futurism, si-
multaneism, paroxysm, impulsionism, the Abbaye group,
the phantasists. Each movement was accompanied by
myriads of avant-garde reviews vying with one another in
an effort to capture the new rhythm of the time. Cendrars
was soon haunting Montparnasse with Modigliani,
Gleizes, and Soutine, having his daily aperitif with Fer-
nand Léger at the corner of the rue de Buci, turning the
"wheels of madness in the gutter of the sky"[14] with
Chagall whom he would cheer up with his laughter,

admiring the Eiffel Tower with Robert Delaunay, getting into hot arguments at the Closerie des Lilas with the poets then in vogue, who were too academic for his taste. At the Bal Bullier he stunned the public with his extravagant American ties, parading with Arthur Cravan and Sonia and Robert Delaunay in a colorful foursome. Cravan wore his shirttails daubed with paint over his slacks and the Delaunays flaunted their multicolored "simultaneous" dresses and tuxedos, setting a fashion the futurist delegate in Paris would cable in every detail to Milan, where such news was advertised as a manifestation of futurism.

There was more in stock for Paris from the paragon of modernity. True to his vocation of fierce independence, Cendrars would not enslave himself to any coterie or school. Although in 1913 and 1914 some of his poems appeared in Apollinaire's *Soirées de Paris*, in Canudo's *Montjoie*, and in *Der Sturm* in Berlin, he became his own promoter, publisher, and printer. After two months' stay in Richard Hall's studio on the rue Lauriston, Cendrars moved to a small hotel in the Latin Quarter where he shared a room with Emil Szittya, founder of the avantgarde German review *Neue Menschen*. Under Cendrars's direction and with the help of a third partner, Marius Hanot, *Les Hommes Nouveaux* became an international Franco-German publishing enterprise, with its headquarters in two attics that the trio had rented at 4, rue de Savoie.

The first issue of *Les Hommes Nouveaux*, in October 1912, featured two poems of "Séquences," uncharacteristic writings of Cendrars's youth, when he was still Freddy Sauser. In the same year, a special issue of sixteen pages presented the famous *Les Pâques*, titled in 1926 "*Les Pâques à New York*." With an incantatory simplicity of form, the poem captures the inner beat and movement of the city which swells into a shatteringly modern spiritual vibration of all humanity at the crossroads of the universe. It eclipsed all other current poetic production. It was a revelation to Apollinaire, marking so sharp a turning point in his own style that the question of mutual influences between the two poets became highly controversial and led to a still unsettled literary dispute among scholars.[15]

Later, in April 1913, again through *Les Hommes Nouveaux*, Cendrars stormed Paris with an even more astonishing creation, the fruit of his international roamings on the railroads of Europe: *La Prose du Transsibérien et de la Petite Jeanne de France.* This work won for him from Dos Passos the epithet, "Homer of the Transsiberian." It is to poetry what the *Bachianas Brasilieras* of Villa-Lobos are to music. It not only evokes, with inimitable rhythm, the romance and the reality of an epic journey on the transsiberian railroad, but it sets the tone of a modern transnational lyricism. At the same time it is the odyssey of the poet in his attempt to capture the prismatic multiple reality of the modern world in its simultaneity and to test the limits of poetry facing the overwhelming universe:

> For I am still a very bad poet
> For the universe overflows me.[16]

La Prose du Transsibérien, announced as the first "simultaneous" book, was a stunning innovation in publishing style and typography. The text was printed in type of various colors and fonts on a folding sheet, two meters long, and illustrated by the "simultaneous" colors of Sonia Delaunay-Terk. Cendrars had 150 copies printed and announced proudly that his poem thus equaled the height of the Eiffel Tower.

Simultaneism was at its zenith in 1913, and *La Prose du Transsibérien* triggered off a series of scathing lampoons—now picaresque, now mean—in the press. Engaged in the polemic were Henri Barzun, who had just published an article on simultaneism in *Poème et drame: Anthologie internationale de la poétique et des idées modernes*, André Salmon from *Gil Blas*, P. Lévy from *Paris-Journal*, D'Antin from *La Liberté*, and many others; to all of them Cendrars answered wittily and scornfully. Proclaiming that simultaneism was purely "pictural" and "representative," expressing itself "technically in depth in raw material,"[17] Cendrars denied any similitude between his technique and Henri Barzun's "schoolish theories of psychological depth." Irritated by all this literary squabbling, Cendrars published in *Der Sturm*, in September 1913, an article denouncing subservience to any movement: "Literature is part of life . . . writing for me is not a job, living is not a job . . . . I denounce the grubbers [*bûcheurs*] and the arrivists. There are no schools."[18]

True to his word, Cendrars avoided all fashions and schools, liberating himself even from the tyranny of poetic liberation which had started to invade Paris, and proceeded with new, independent experiments. Although *Le Panama et les Aventures de mes sept oncles* was not published until 1918, it was conceived and written between June 1913 and June 1914 and announced: "Poetry starts today." It has been considered by critics as Cendrars's most original poem, almost achieving the impossible in poetry through the sheer force of the word disintegrated and disconnected from emotional charges. Nevertheless, Cendrars was to bring about further innovations in his enterprise of purging poetic techniques with *Dix-neuf poèmes élastiques*. All these poems were also written in 1913-14, as their appearance in various reviews in France and abroad proves, but they were not published as a collection in Paris until 1919. The year 1913 has recently been singled out as the first year of the twentieth century.[19] For Cendrars the century had started long before 1913, but he was undoubtedly in the forefront at his official birth, stretching to its extreme the modern disjunction of form and reality.

Meanwhile, the "hero of our time" was pursuing his richly variegated life in the throes of poverty and amid poignant inner struggles. After only three issues, *Les Hommes Nouveaux* was discontinued. To make a living, Cendrars opened at the journal's headquarters an international translation office, and continued to write, under his own name and under various pseudonyms, countless articles for various magazines on painting, Russian music, and literature.

In May 1913 Fela returned from New York. She and Cendrars settled into the two attics on the rue de Savoie which Cendrars kept for several years, just to store things between trips while experimenting with life in other sections of Paris and in its suburbs. At that time his correspondence shows him with Fela in Saint-Cloud, Sèvres, Ville-d'Avray, Les Forges en Barbizon, and Saint-Martin-en-Bière. At Les Forges he left Fela and his first son, named Odilon in honor of the painter, to answer the "call to foreigners, friends of France," and enlist in the Foreign Legion. In September 1914, before leaving, he married Fela. A second son, Rémy, was born in 1915, but Cendrars was too much at grips with the world, with life, with his own creative, devouring fire, to be a family man, and he gradually disappeared from Fela's life.

During the war he underwent a severe ordeal which, if far from curbing his writer's talent, would radically alter his destiny as a man and sharpen his character. During a battle in the Marne Valley on September 26, 1915, the day of Rémy de Gourmont's death (which Cendrars considered an omen), a bombshell shattered his right forearm; fearing gangrene, he himself cut off the hanging hand. He was taken to a hospital in Paris where his arm was amputated above the elbow. Throughout his life he suffered recurring and severe bouts of pain and felt as if the missing hand were still there:

> That is my star
> It is shaped like a hand
> That is my hand gone up to heaven
> . . . .
> . . . that hand
> which must feel pain
> Just like my amputated hand hurts pierced as it is
> by a continuous sting.[20]

APOCALYPTIC FRENZY OF CREATIVE EXORCISM, 1916-1924

The war experience left Cendrars practically destitute. Although his inner self was in spiritual disarray, and he was more than ever torn between the downward pull of Schopenhauer's pessimism, which had always attracted him, and his own indomitable energy and exaltation of being, he plunged once more into the quick of life.

After a short time in Cannes and Nice with Fela, Cendrars returned to Paris determined to learn how to write with his left hand. He evokes in *Bourlinguer* the drinking sessions he used to have with Modigliani in Montparnasse, when people off the street would invite the crippled man to have a drink but would not pay for his lunch. He met once again his old painter friends, Léger, Picabia, and Braque, and made a few new acquaintances: Erik Satie, Max Jacob, Aragon, Desnos, Soupault. Soupault recalls Cendrars's extraordinary presence in 1917, with his dazzling enthusiasm and his usual lucidity, but also his tension: "Eyes wide open, Blaise Cendrars tried to understand the upheavals that were to occur," yet "I felt he was disquieted, sometimes irritated. He wanted to travel and—one thing does not prevent the other—to isolate himself."[21]

Indeed, Cendrars did not remain confined to Paris. If international wanderings on transcontinental trains and sea voyages were temporarily out of bounds, he still found a way to satisfy his insatiable curiosity for human variety among the eternal travelers, the "gens du voyage" of the gypsy world. Through Sawo, a gypsy friend he met in the Foreign Legion, Cendrars was introduced to his "Gitan" tribe and roamed the suburbs of Paris gathering the stories he wrote thirty years later and published in *Rhapsodies Gitanes*. The 1916 gypsy interlude also introduced him to the little village of Méréville, in Beauce, where he pretended to have made the fortune of the local pharmacist by inventing a process of making salt out of watercress. At any rate, when he was not off in Cannes or Nice, the old barn in Méréville gave him the retreat he needed to escape from the literary jungle of Paris, until he found more congenial headquarters in Le Tremblay sur Mauldre, next to friends like the actor Marcel Lévesque and the painter Francis Picabia.

After composing *La Guerre au Luxembourg*, a model of irony at the glorious elation infused even into children's games by the war climate, Cendrars wrote *Profond Aujourd'hui* in 1917. "Impaled on his sensitivity," he capsulizes in this short essay the frantic disintegrated and yet totalizing consciousness of today, in a breathless, intense poetic prose that seems both an optimistic hymn to modernity and a lucid disclosure of its destructive powers at work. Soon afterward he wrote *J'ai tué*, a vigorous and relentless condemnation of war which resounds with the quick percussive heartbeat of a man quartered in the trenches and ends in a characteristic grip on life: "I have the sense of reality, I, a poet. I acted. I killed, as someone who wants to live."[22]

At the same time Cendrars was working on two of his most original productions: *La fin du monde filmée par l'ange Notre-Dame* and *L'Eubage*.[23] No subsequent surrealist prose or modern creations of science fiction has equaled the apocalyptic cosmic irony of these two models of postmodern[24] poetic prose, in which Cendrars appears as much a master of the word as a visionary prophet of our times.

It is noteworthy that throughout these crucial years Cendrars was gradually weaving his past experience of revolutions, wars, spiritual and physical agony and struggle, together with a prescience of global destruction, into the most mind- and soul-shattering hero-monster phenomenon created in the century: Moravagine. The novel was not published until 1926, but excerpts appeared in 1921. *La fin du monde* had been intended as the third part of *Moravagine*, and the character had been haunting Cendrars since before the war. As Jacques-Henry Lévesque first noted, *Moravagine* is to a certain extent the epitome of the Dada spirit. With his usual almost supernatural sensitivity to his time, Cendrars caught in it the spiritual and psychological disintegration of the age, the violence, the erotic perversion, the victory of the irrational, the diabolical destructive orgy that sweeps through the world as does the eery, at times satanic, at times irresponsible laughter of the hero Moravagine. The novel was a devastating, anticipatory embodiment of the individual and collective schizophrenia that was to contaminate the twentieth century.

Although caught in the wake of a frenzy of creative exorcism, Cendrars did not become its prisoner. He alternated a solitary life in his countryside retreat with increasing personal involvements in the Paris world. The year 1917 had not only been a decisive turning point in his life as a writer; it was also the year of the deepest determining change in his personal life. He had just been introduced to the young actress Raymone Duchâteau, who was to become his lifelong companion and, in 1949, his second wife.

By 1919 Cendrars was extremely active on the Paris artistic and literary scene. In that year his previously mentioned poems were published in book form. It was also the year of his collaboration at the *Rose Rouge,* when he wrote his series of epoch-making articles on the painters Braque, Chagall, and Delaunay, and on cubism— announcing the "disintegration of the cube."

Still interested in renovating the art of publishing, Cendrars also collaborated with Paul Laffite at Éditions de la Sirène, outlining an ambitious program for more than 200 volumes. He edited a vast collection of the *Mémoires* of Casanova; he planned translations of Stevenson and of Alexandrian and Byzantine novels, reeditions of Lautréamont, Baudelaire, Villon, and Nerval, and an anthology of the Paris of Balzac, together with productions of his own, such as *La fin du monde* and *L'anthologie nègre,* which he published in 1921. The latter is another example of the versatility and universality of Cendrars's interests. African arts were becoming fashionable in France at the time, but Cendrars was the first writer to recognize the seminal importance of African languages and literatures. With his usual gargantuan bibliomania and his addiction to punctilious research, he assembled a solidly representative collection of African tales with an extensive bibliography.

During the same years, always in the front seat on the wheel of time, Cendrars developed a passion for cinematographic arts. He wrote *L'A B C du cinéma,* which, like most of his writings appeared in several publications between 1919 and 1921 before it came out in completed form in 1926. In 1919 he met the film director, Abel Gance, and entered actively into film production. He was first a stand-in in the war film *J'accuse,* and in 1920-21 he collaborated with Gance on the famous avant-garde film *La Roue,* described by Fernand Léger as the "first French film which managed to individualize the object and the fragment of the object,"[25] a typically Cendrarian quality.

Cendrars pursued his cinematographic experiments in Rome, directing a film for the studio Rinascimento, *La Vénus Noire*, featuring the Indian dancer Dourga. Although the film was never released, the publication of its scenario, *La perle fiévreuse*, gives an idea of the originality of Cendrars's goals for this new art form. After this last engagement with the Rome studios, which, according to Cendrars, was interrupted by Mussolini's push on Rome, he is supposed to have been sent to the upper Sudan to prepare a documentary film on the life of elephants. The poems presented in this volume under the heading "Elephant Hunting" seem to authenticate the African trip.

Poetry, essays, novels, art criticism, publishing innovations, film arts could not entirely contain the versatile and voracious genius of Cendrars. He applied his talents to the multiple art of the opera and wrote a scenario for the Swedish Ballet directed by Rolf de Maré; *La création du Monde*, an African version of the creation of the world. The ballet was presented on October 25, 1923, at the Théâtre des Champs Elysées with music by Darius Milhaud, choreography by Jean Borlin, and costumes and stage scenery designed by Fernand Léger.

In spite of his rich inner and outer life, increasing restlessness assailed Cendrars. Time and again he would say, in his later writings and interviews, that he was not a career writer and had always felt there was more to life than writing books. In 1923 he met the Brazilian writer Oswaldo de Andrade and helped to launch his wife, the painter Tarsila, in the Paris art world. Irritated and disgruntled by the dictatorial turn that literature took in Paris with emerging surrealism, Cendrars accepted de Andrade's invitation to São Paulo; he "grabbed the chance and hurried off . . . only too happy to break away from the chores and the commercialism of the Parisian public demonstrations in which poetry was confined."[26]

SOUTH AMERICAN JOURNEYS,
1924-1928

"At le Tremblay sur Mauldre (Seine-et-Oise) the N.10 highway goes by my door. . . . Who knows the N.10 highway from beginning to end, from the steps of Notre Dame to its terminal point on the other side of the Atlantic, beyond the Iguassú and up to the Rio Paraná?"[27] Thus Cendrars later evoked his commuting years between France and South America, from his "house in the fields" in Le Tremblay, his main retreat until World War II when it was ransacked during the German occupation.

Brazil, which he considered his second motherland, was a country after Cendrars's own heart, with its buoyant modern dynamism, its pagan mythologies, its mobile cultural variety, the piercing and stirring way in which it sets the mind on edge. Not only did he bring back from these transatlantic sailings the *Ocean Letters* (*Feuilles de route*) presented in this volume, but later in his life South America became a recurrent theme enlarging the already wide range of the sources of his inspiration. Those commentators who have expressed doubt as to the reality of Cendrars's travels should be convinced by the fact that at least three of his visits to Brazil were recorded in Rio de Janeiro and São Paulo newspapers.

On February 6, 1924, Cendrars arrived in Rio on board the SS *Formosa*. Soon he went on to São Paulo where, ironically enough, he was greeted by another circle of activist-modernists who, in spite of having declared willful independence from European influences, were imitating Paris. Through Oswaldo de Andrade, Cendrars met all the Paulist *modernistos*: Tasto di Almeida, Couto do Barros, Rubens de Moraes, Luiz Aranha, Antonio de Alcantara Machado, Mario Andrade, and Paulo Prado, author of *Retrato do Brazil*. Prado remained Cendrars's friend until his death in 1943. In a lecture at the Correo Paulistano on February 22, 1924, Cendrars announced to his startled audience that the days of literature were over: "Nous ne faisons plus de littérature."[28] Today this pronouncement may sound like an echo from Dada's bombshells, but for Cendrars it had been an article of faith since 1912. In May 1924 he gave another lecture at the Villa Kirial de Freitas Valle on African literature and in June he spoke to the *modernistos* in São Paulo on poetry and linguistics. This lecture proved once again how far ahead of his time he already was, for the subject of linguistics had only recently begun to claim the attention of a nonspecialized public. René de Saussure had lectured in Geneva between 1906 and 1911, and Cendrars might well have attended some of his courses.

During his first stay in Brazil, Cendrars made many exploratory forays into the country and roamed around the *favelás* of Rio, where he frightened his hosts but made friends among the natives, who called him "the kind one-armed little Frenchman."[29] He managed to be taken to the far end of the Minas Gerais district, where he was deeply moved by the sculptures of the little cripple Aleijadinho. He brought back hoards of stories, real and imaginary, such as that of Manolo Seca, the owner of the last gas station in the *sertão* who carved the Stations of the Cross around his garage, each character featured in an automobile.

A card to Tarsila, mailed from Le Tremblay on October 25, 1924, reveals that Cendrars was back in France by that date. Probably stimulated by his recent explorations, he published his earlier travel poems on North America, *Kodak (Documentaire)*, and the first part of *Feuilles de route*, "Le Formose," about his transatlantic crossing to South America, both later presented in this volume.

Cendrars seems to have stayed in Le Tremblay through 1925, a year of intensive writing to judge by the publications that followed. The publisher Grasset launched the novel *L'Or* (*Sutter's Gold*), the story of John Augustus Sutter which brought instant fame to Cendrars. Although many previous and subsequent works of Cendrars are more striking in originality and depth, *Sutter's Gold* achieves a kind of perfection in a terse direct blend of imaginative and historical narrative. With his usual empathy for lands and people, Cendrars not only dramatized Sutter's pathetic destiny but turned the California adventure into an allegory of man's destruction through the lure of wealth and technology. In 1925, the year of publication, the novel came out in German and Czechoslovakian, to be followed by translation into English (1926), Hungarian (1927), and Russian and Italian (1929). In the end, forty-five editions appeared in ten different languages, with six reprints in German, two in Italian, and five in Spanish.

Cendrars was now well launched. In 1926 Grasset published the famous *Moravagine*, reprinted eight times before its inclusion in the complete works. It was also translated into German, Spanish, and English. *L'Eubage*, mentioned earlier, finally came out at the Sans Pareil publishing house, while Les Ecrivains Réunis gathered the various articles on films into *L'A B C du cinéma* and also published a short essay with the title *Éloge de la vie dangereuse* (*In Praise of Dangerous Life*). A typically Cendrarian piece, the essay starts with a high-tension meditation on solitude in the tropical forests, which leads to metaphysical considerations on the lack of unity: "There is no unity. . . . There is no absolute. Therefore there is no truth, except absurd life flapping its donkey's ears."[30] It goes on to relate the story of a criminal Cendrars met in a prison he visited on Easter Sunday.

Cendrars brought back this phantasmagoric essay from

his second trip to Brazil, which he had made in the spring of 1926 at Paulo Prado's invitation. Filippo Marinetti, then in São Paulo, was scheduled to deliver a lecture on May 19. Aracy A. Amaral gives a detailed account of the rather bristling encounter between the two writers.[31] When demonstrations against him prevented Marinetti from reaching the lecture hall, Cendrars declared it showed the good taste of the Paulists, a comment that is not surprising since Cendrars had always despised the theories of the futurists, whom he considered puerile. Cendrars was back in France by June 1926, but he returned to Brazil in 1927 and probably visited it once more in 1928, although there is no factual evidence of this last trip. In the meantime, the poems that constitute the second and third parts of *Feuilles de route* (*Ocean Letters*) appeared gradually in different reviews, and *Petits contes nègres pour les enfants des Blancs*, a sequel to *Anthologie nègre* which he announced in the poem "Luggage," came out in 1928.

VOYAGE TO THE ANTIPODES OF THE MIND, 1927-1930

While the Brazilian experience fulfilled the love of action in a man who could have been the spiritual father of the Beat wanderers, Cendrars had simultaneously undertaken another kind of voyage. During his vagabond hotel life in Paris, his hops to Le Tremblay, and a prolonged retreat in La Redonne near Marseille in 1927, he completed his next major novel, *Dan Yack* which he published in 1929 in two parts: *Le Plan de l'aiguille* and *Les Confessions de Dan Yack*.

Like *Moravagine*, *Dan Yack* had been maturing in Cendrars's imagination ever since the war. As early as 1919 he announced the volume in a dedicatory note to Abel Gance: "Do not look in it for a new art formula, for a

new mode of narrative discourse, but actually for the
expression of tomorrow's state of mind."[32] Although this
statement could be made of almost all Cendrars's writ-
ings, *Dan Yack* is definitely a landmark in his literary
production. It was probably his last piece of creative
exorcism and his final coming to terms with the world's
and his own divided self.

Dan Yack, falling outside all the standard categories of
the art of the novel, baffled the critics. Being not only of
his time, but being his time, Cendrars had gone beyond
his contemporaries. At first reading, *Dan Yack* is not
unlike Poe's *The Narrative of Arthur Gordon Pym*, at
least in *Le Plan de l'aiguille*. This part may be read on the
surface as a tale of adventure on a voyage to the Antarctic
with the gruesome saga of an experimental settlement of
four men alone with a dog in a polar island and the
unbelievable success story of the establishment of a
multinational whale trading company in a futuristic
settlement which Dan Yack symptomatically names
"Community City." In the second part, *Les Confessions
de Dan Yack*, there is apparently a startling collapse of
creative tension. After the last episode of the Antarctic
fugue Dan Yack had been caught in the grim reality of
war and had abandoned his megalomaniac dreams for the
almost supernatural platonic love of a young girl named
Mireille. We now find him, after Mireille's unaccountable
death, isolated in an Alpine chalet. In a manner that
anticipates Beckett's *Krapp's Last Tape*, Dan Yack tries to
tape his memories and pages from Mireille's diary. In this
attempt the will to live or the will to be is transformed
into the urge to speak the word that cannot be spoken. In
spite of its seemingly anticlimatic nature the *Confessions
of Dan Yack* adds another dimension to the adventures of
Le Plan de l'aiguille. *Dan Yack* actually appears as a
voyage to the antipodes of modern consciousness, antici-
pating, with the demise of the individual and his tech-

Blaise Cendrars

Feuilles de route

I.

le Formose

Dessins de Tarsila

Au Sans Pareil

27, avenue Klüber

PARIS

1 9 2 4

The cover of the original edition of *Feuilles de route:
le Formose*. Drawing by Tarsila.

Cendrars, by Fernand Léger, 1919 (from *J'ai tué*). [Copyright by SPADEM, Paris (Société de la propriété artistique et des dessins et modèles)]

Cendrars, by Francis Picabia, 1924 (from *Kodak*).
[Copyright ADAGP and SPADEM, Paris]

Blaise Cendrars (sitting at the left of the central row) at the Ecole de Commerce, Neuchâtel, in 1904. [Collection Raymone Cendrars—Editions Denoël, Paris]

Cendrars in his Foreign Legion uniform, 1915. [Collection
Raymone Cendrars—Editions Denoël, Paris]

Cendrars in 1934. [Collection of
Mme. Jacques-Henry Lévesque]

Cendrars in the garden of Saint-Segond, 1949. [Collection of Mme. Jacques-Henry Lévesque]

Blaise Cendrars and Jacques-Henry Lévesque on the rue Jean Dolent in Paris, 1950. [Collection of Mme. Jacques-Henry Lévesque]

Blaise and Raymone Cendrars with their dog Wagon-lit in the garden of Saint-Segond, Villefranche-sur-Mer, 1949. [Collection Raymone Cendrars—Editions Denoël, Paris]

nological sway over the world, the structuralist vision of the new ecologists of the mind, which Robert Scholes has recently assessed in his analysis of the structural imagination.[33]

With this semi-autobiographical, semiphantasmagoric allegorical tale, Cendrars reaches a cybernetic concept of fiction which places him in the forefront of the structural revolution of the novel. As early as 1929, with *Dan Yack*, he was fulfilling the standards for the novel of the future, as defined by Anaïs Nin in 1968, spanning all chasms between reality and unreality. If the personality distortions of Moravagine in his psychiatric ward, to the extent of identifying himself with a nail in the wall, make Roquentin's gropings for the reality of existence in Sartre's *Nausea* look pale by comparison, Dan Yack's fantastic symphony of the New World makes the hallucinating depersonalizations of man in war or the megamarkets of Le Clezio seem like linguistic exercises.

In the vortex of this spell of orphic creativity, Cendrars paused for a moment of meditative self-evaluation and self-depreciation which he records in his first fragment of autobiography, *Une nuit dans la forêt*. Taking the measure of the vanity of action, which he considered the absolute form of contempt for life, and disclosing the illusionary nature of freedom, long before the existentialists he diagnosed the serenity of despair. He saw it as the "last state of wisdom,"[34] and lucidly identified himself as a "Brahman in reverse" (*Brahmane à rebours*)[35] a much-quoted phrase which epitomizes Cendrars's multi-dimensional nature.

When reading this moving "Confession of a Child of a Century," one cannot agree more with the sharp intuitive comment of Henry Miller, who warned that "to use the word 'cosmic' with reference to him [Cendrars] would be to insult him; it would imply he accepted life."[36] On his return from this Antarctic journey of the mind, Cendrars, who had lived the megalomania of destruction with Moravagine and of construction with Dan Yack, knew that "serenity can be achieved only by a desperate mind" and that "to know despair, one must have lived a great deal and still love the world."[37] For Cendrars there was no barrier between cosmic and worldly consciousness and no hierarchy; there was only equal love and scorn for all the grandeur and all the misery of being, whatever antipodes he could reach.

THE WORLD REPORTER, 1930-1940

In comparison with the preceding years, the decade of the 1930s was a period of creative lull for Cendrars. He seemed temporarily to desert the realm of the imaginary for the world of "true stories," journalistic reporting, and translations.

The writer, however, prevailed over the journalist. Commissioned by the illustrated weekly *Vu* to write the story of the adventurer Jean Galmot, who was then being tried in court at Nantes, Cendrars turned out a piece of true biographical literature, *Rhum*. Galmot, gold-seeker, trapper, rum dealer, a deputy in Guiana, the victim of political intrigues, imprisoned and finally poisoned just as he returned to Guiana for a new term as deputy, was, like, Sutter, a personality suited to Cendrars's fascination for the success and failure stories of those who tempt destiny. At the same time, launching a new publishing venture with a collection entitled *Les Têtes Brûlées*, he characteristically chose to adapt the stories of two non-conformists, the diplomat-vagrant Lieutenant Bringolf and the famous Chicago gangster Al Capone.

Between 1930 and 1935 Cendrars's correspondence reveals vagabond wanderings in the Alfa Romeo designed by Braque, which the one-armed poet had already been driving for years at breakneck speed. One finds Cendrars in Toulon, in Hyères, gathering grapes from Toulon to Biarritz, in Le Tremblay of course, and probably in countless other places. In Biarritz he frequently stayed at the home of Eugenia Errazuris, the famous South American patron of artists, dreaming of jaunts to Portugal and occasionally realizing his wish. At one point he wrote to John Dos Passos that he was getting ready to leave for China. He was expecting a journalistic assignment there, but, unfortunately for himself and for his readers, his lifelong dream did not materialize.

After publishing another Africa-inspired tale, *Comment les Blancs sont d'anciens Noirs* (1930), and gathering several earlier essays into the volume entitled *Aujourd'hui* (1931), Cendrars wrote, for *Les Cahiers Romands*, the story of his childhood escape, *Vol à Voile* (1932). In 1935 he brought out *Panorama de la pègre*, a collection of documentary reports he had written on the underworlds of Paris, Marseille, and London for the Paris daily *Le Jour*.

In the next two years the undefatigable sea rover crossed the ocean twice to the United States. Later, expressing his love for New York to his radio interviewer Michel Manoll, Cendrars boasted that he had sailed to New York nine times in 1938. The records of the Compagnie Générale Transatlantique show that he was a guest of honor on the maiden voyage of the SS *Normandie* between May 29 and June 3, 1935. In 1936 *Paris Soir* sent Cendrars to Hollywood as a special reporter. His articles were published in book form the same year: *Hollywood: La Mecque du cinéma*. Here again we find his characteristic visionary empathy for things and people: "A reporter is not merely a picture hunter; he must know how to capture the mind's reality."[38]

Before his departure for Hollywood Cendrars had adapted the book of the famous outlaw Al Jennings,

Through the Shadows with O'Henry. The French translation, *Hors la Loi*, was subsequently published in Flemish and Portuguese versions and apparently brought fame to its poor old outcast author. In his radio interviews with Michel Manoll, Cendrars recalled with emotion his meeting in Hollywood with Jennings, a puny, agitated, clear-eyed seventy-year-old man, who gave Cendrars one of his guns as a souvenir.

Cendrars sailed back to Europe on a freighter via the Panama Canal. As far as is known, that was his last long sea voyage. On his return he published two series of short stories, *Histoires vraies* and *La vie dangereuse*. Weaving into them characters, events, and scenes from his multifarious experiences, both real and imaginary, he once again took his readers across continents and into different cultures, from the Paris suburbs to Vancouver, the Amazon, the *favelás* in Rio, and the stormy seas, bringing to life a galaxy of exotic characters, ranging from unknown saints to criminals. His fascination with South America was revived in his translation of Ferreira de Castro's novel, *A Selva*, a successful publication launched in 1938 and reprinted five times. Brazil also inspired Cendrars to write one of his best collection of short stories, *D'Oultremer à indigo*, in which he gave free rein to a neobaroque style of magic realism.

World War II stalled the Homeric storyteller. The Brazilian short stories went almost unnoticed in the rumbles of the war. In the spring of 1940 Cendrars used his reporting talents as a war correspondent in the English army for a number of provincial newspapers, but the volume derived from that experience was destroyed by the Germans; it did, however, reach the public in 1964 when his complete works were published. After relinquishing the reportorial job, Cendrars withdrew to Aix-en-Provence where, shattered by another world cataclysm which was going to deprive him of his younger son,

Rémy, a pilot whose plane crashed in Morocco in 1945, he resolutely renounced literature—forever, he thought.

CONTEMPLATIVE RECOLLECTION OF THINGS PAST: A NEW SURGE OF CREATIVITY, 1943-1949

In a small furnished apartment on the rue Clemenceau in Aix-en-Provence, Cendrars entered into a phase of total silence. For three years of intense concentration the "Brahman in reverse" withdrew into a kind of mental levitation. His lifelong interest, since reading Rémy de Gourmont's *Latin Mystique* as an adolescent, in the heightened consciousness of saints and mystics was revivified in this solitary retreat, where the library in Aix, like the libraries of Saint Petersburg, Rome, and New York, provided nourishment for his meditation. He devoured the *Patrologiae* of Migne, Jean de Bolland's *Acta Sanctorum*, and numerous other collections, read the Bible in its entirety, and again became immersed in his favorite mystics, Saint John of the Cross and Teresa de Avila. Cendrars's reclusion, partly caused by the war, partly self-imposed, proved to have been a fecund period of spiritual and intellectual renewal which fulfilled the contemplative facet of his multiple nature.

In fact, the fire was slumbering under the embers and needed but a slight touch of the poker to spark it anew. "And then I caught fire in my solitude, for writing is to burn oneself out,"[39] Cendrars wrote to his friend Édouard Peisson, recalling his visit on the morning of August 21, 1943. That same night he settled down at his typewriter in the kitchen, the only room he could heat in his freezing apartment, and let the flow of his memories pour until the small hours of the morning, planning another ten years of creative insomnia. Starting with war recollections, his years in Marseille and La Redonne, and his life with the gypsies in *L'Homme foudroyé* (1945), evoking

more war scenes and companions in *La Main coupée*
(1946), Cendrars wound up the account of his trans-
European wanderings in *Bourlinguer* (1948). In September
of that year he moved to Saint-Segond, a dreamlike estate
in Villefranche. There he completed his autobiographical
tetralogy in the mystic effusions of the life of Saint Joseph
of Cupertino, "the new patron saint of aviation" who
knew how to fly backward in levitation, and in the trans-
planetary visions of "La Tour Eiffel sidérale." These two
pieces were published as *Le Lotissement du ciel* (1949).

In these four volumes, a modernized form of the
Proustian quest, Cendrars renewed and revitalized the
autobiographical genre, recapturing his past and reflect-
ing on the mechanisms of literary creation. Like Proust,
but a Proust of the twenty-first century realizing a very
different fusion of past, present, and future, Cendrars
knew that not memory alone but a transmuting power is
at work which makes the past an eternal present and
performs the miracle of an enhanced vision. He recalled
"in [his] insomnias the unforgettable past and its deceiv-
ing, fallacious, lying, perspective, and yet miraculous at
the same time, because it is not memory alone which is
awakened and starts to function automatically, but the
eyes, the eyes of childhood that open up, and for the first
time and in a harsh light that sets everything off."[40]

The sixty-year-old globe-trotter had now completed his
spiritual journey from "the entire world to the core of the
world."[41] As Jacques-Henry Lévesque, referring to
Cendrars's poetry, first pointed out, Cendrars through
constant renewal achieved the junction of the absolute
and the relative and captured the permanence of the
instant. Cendrars, however, differs from Proust. A work
of art has for him no finality; it is an open form that
invites one to explore a continuous space. Eroticism and
mysticism coexist in a complex and contradictory uni-
verse, where all things take on equal significance as non-

privileged components of reality. The creation of the writer is not only a semiology of the world; it is essentially a springboard to open-ended reverie and meditation. His style changed accordingly, taking on the amplitude of a continuous uncurbed flow of long-winding periods drifting through the wealth of his experience. Cendrars himself provides the best analysis of the novelty of his Einsteinian technique: "I type and type, . . . inserting into the direct vision the reflective one that can be deciphered only in reverse as in a mirror, master of my life, controlling time, having managed to disjoint and dislocate it, and slipping relativity like a substratum into my sentences, thus making it the very spring of my writing technique."[42] Once again Cendrars innovates and renovates. A completely developed theory of postmodern narratology underlies his autobiographical tetralogy.

RETURN TO PARIS: THE LAST YEARS, 1949-1961

The calm, sunny, subtropical gardens of Saint-Segond seemed to be the ideal setting for Cendrars's intensive creative recollection, but they were soon invaded by his importunate admirers. In 1949, now a widower, Cendrars married Raymone Duchâteau in the village of Sigriswil in Switzerland, and with her he left Villefranche for the turbulent Paris.

In the Paris of the 1950s the once-rebellious poet was acclaimed and received triumphantly. His tetralogy achieved instant fame. His poems had been published in a complete edition, with a brilliant and perceptive introduction by Jacques-Henry Lévesque. Critical studies and special issues of major reviews were devoted to him; a series of radio interviews revived the legendary world-roaming author for French audiences; selections from his earlier works were published. Cendrars, having lost his cherished independence, belonged at last to the public. In

1958 the writer who had held all officialdom in contempt received the literary prize of the Ville de Paris, and André Malraux came to his apartment to laurel him commander of the Legion of Honor.

Meanwhile, Cendrars was still listing thirty-three books in preparation, a figure he had chosen to announce throughout his life because it is considered a magic key to activity. He had actually been working on one of the novels mentioned in his list, "La Carrissima," the story of Mary Magdalene, which he foresaw as the greatest love story ever written. Unfortunately, he never completed that project, but his creative energy never flagged. He published a documentary analysis of Brazil, *Le Brésil, des hommes sont venus* (1952). In 1953, with the collaboration of Nino Frank, he created and broadcast a program of Christmas stories, *Noël aux quatre coins de monde*, and in the following years he wrote three plays for the radio on characteristic topics—*Serajevo, Gilles de Rais*, and *Le divin Aretin*—which were published in 1959 under the title *Films sans images*. The "films without pictures" brought a new dimension to the genre, blending the poetic atmosphere of legend and relentless psychological realism with pungent, vigorous language. From this work it would seem that Cendrars could easily have revolutionized the art of the theater, if he had chosen to devote his talents to playwriting.

But this "horseman of the apocalypse," as Raymond Dumay called him,[43] had other ways to lash the theater world and stun the Paris public avid for flesh-creeping stories. In 1956 the author of *Moravagine* outdid himself, reaching beyond the atrocities of a Céline or a Genet to the ultimate in physical and psychological horror in *Emmène-moi au bout du monde*. On the surface, this wrathful, violent novel, the story of a prurient aging actress possessed of a frantic hypervitality, slashes through the rotting fabric of Parisian society. Cendrars mischievously announces in a nota bene preceding the story, that it is a roman à clef, and he hopes that no one will be "inelegant enough to try to disclose any clue, the clues of deceit." And indeed it would be idle and aesthetically false to reduce this phantasmagoric vision of horror to mere reality. The novel can be seen, however, as a scream of rage, a revolt of the mind and spirit against the decay of the flesh, from a man of indomitable vital energy who was soon to face physical deterioration and death. Not long afterward, paralysis struck the enraged writer, but *Emmène-moi au bout du monde* was not to be his swan song. A year later a collection of short stories gathered together the last memories of this "inexhaustible creative substance"[44] under the revealing title, *Trop c'est trop* (*Too Much Is Too Much*).

In January 1961 Cendrars died in a first-floor apartment on the rue José Maria de Heredia, where Raymone had taken him at the beginning of his illness. Missing from his logbook was the trip to the moon he had been anticipating for the past fifty years, as he had humorously put it a few years before: "For the last fifty years I have been once a year to the famous travel agency on Place de la Madeleine to book again my seat on the first journey to the Moon."[45]

A NEW GENRE: VERBAL SNAPSHOTS AND POSTCARDS

In the midst of the innumerable articles, short stories, pieces of sidereal prose, and novels that Cendrars published in the twenties, the poems *Documentaires*, *Feuilles de route* (*Ocean Letters*), and *Sud-Américaines* (*South American Women*) were overshadowed and too willingly considered as his farewell to poetry, a weak bounce of his pre–World War I poetic inspiration.

Walter Albert, who presented to English-speaking readers Cendrars's complete earlier poems, with a few selections from the later experiments, even finds "a disintegration of the power, vigor and beauty of his best verse" in "the flat undemanding prose poetry of *Documentaires* and *Feuilles de route*."[46] On the other hand, John Dos Passos felt so attuned to the strains of these songs of the road and sea that as early as 1931 he added selections from them to his translation of *Le Panama ou les Aventures de mes sept oncles*. Similarly, the French poet, novelist, and worldwide traveler, Paul Morand, was charmed by Cendrars's "cumulative inventory of the globe" and by the Whitmanesque echoes of those "microcosms" that "sweep the planet with their searchlights."[47] Heir not only to Whitman but to the Victorine sequential poetry of the monks of Saint-Gall, as Charles Albert Cingria has noted in *La civilisation de Saint-Gall*,[48] Cendrars gradually broke away from the confinement of all poetic structures and metrics and created in his last poems a style that could be considered the prototype of the modern renewal of sequential poetry.

The poems in this volume appear for the first time in their entire sequence in the English language. Their unity comes not only from the common theme of North and South American travels, which had already inspired Cendrars to write *Pâques à New York* and *Panama*, but also from the new "postcard" technique that characterizes the last stage in the process of purification to which Cendrars submitted the poetic idiom. Hence the English title chosen for this collection.

Since the lyrical burst *Pâques à New York* and the rhythmic innovations of the *Prose du Transsibérien*, Cendrars had been experimenting with a new aesthetics. He was seeking to free poetry from traditional molds and adjust it to the imperatives of a modern era; like Fernand Léger, he understood that "the eye . . . controls the individual more than ever."[49] As early as *Dix-neuf poèmes élastiques*, in "Aux cinq coins," written in February 1914, Cendrars had already asked defiantly, "I don't know how to open my eyes?" And concluded on the warning that "Poetry is at stake." From then on, with the "windows of [his] poetry wide open on the boulevards"[50] and stripping his poems of all literary artifice, he invented a new art of seeing.

Practicing a Zen-like discipline of concentration, he captured in *Poèmes élastiques* the simultaneous reality of modern contrasts. His swift, alert, trained, and intuitive eye seized with incredible "elasticity" lights, sounds, movements, and static and mobile scenes in a four-dimensional range of vision. But the visual "elasticity" is also a mental and spiritual one, which both accelerates and immobilizes thought in a Western form of satori through the highly developed art of the poetic ellipse. Usually considered the prototype of simultaneist and cubic vision in poetry, *Poèmes élastiques* evinced awareness of the new mode of thought which Deleuze and Guattari would define fifty years later as characteristic of the era of multiplicity.

In 1917, however, Cendrars decided to renounce poetry, convinced that "the poetry then prevalent in Paris seemed to become the foundation of a spiritual misunderstanding and a mental confusion which . . . would poison and paralyze all the activities of the French nation before it spreads to the rest of the world."[51] For Cendrars, poetic liberation could not be achieved through verbal systematization; it had to emerge from the multitudinous reality of the world on which he knew how to focus the telescopic lens of his mind. He therefore carried his technique further in *Documentaires*, which he significantly described in radio interviews as "mental photographs," possibly creating a new genre, as he ironically put it in the foreword to the reprints of the poems, entitled "Document." By that time he probably knew that, four years after publication of *Documentaires*, then called *Kodak*,

Paul Morand had brought out a series of poems on the United States with the subtitle: "Album of Lyrical Photographs."

What Cendrars's mental camera photographed was not actual lands or people, or even the scenery of his imagination, but a continent of words. In *L'Homme foudroyé* he baffled his readers by disclosing that *Documentaires* did not consist of his own travel impressions, but rather was a collation of passages he had cut out of Gustave Lerouge's novel, *Le mystérieux Docteur Cornélius.*[52] Since Lerouge had fallen into oblivion, few people paid attention to Cendrars's revelation. In 1967, however, Francis Lacassin, who introduced the reprint of the forgotten storyteller's serial, took Cendrars at his word, studied the two texts closely, and proved that forty-one poems in *Documentaires* were carved out of Lerouge's prose.[53]

The American reader of *Documentaires* will find it difficult to credit the disclosure about Lerouge when he sees the typically Cendrarian synesthetic sensitivity with which the inner reality of the American continent is captured in all its human and geographical diversity. New York multimillionaires in their posh offices; the Hudson River hustle-bustle; the specificity of a wooden bridge construction; character vignettes of a Mexican-American dancer or an old Indian woman; the leisure-luxury lifestyle on a plantation; the stifling pest-ridden atmosphere of the South, the slumbering power of the Mississippi River—all come alive with vividness, accuracy, and inevitability which no mere verbal play could achieve. Unmistakable and pervasive in *Documentaires* is the poet's individualizing seizure of things in their totality which had earlier marked Freddy Sauser's first impressions of New York as recorded in his diary:

> The ocean widens out like an arena. On its sides, three islands outline the entrances. The Hudson is a track neatly raked. The skyscrapers circle it in tiers. Above, the clouds

are swollen into a multicolored festive tent. Twilight
flashes are the lanterns.
The Statue of Liberty gives the conductor's signal and
the bugle band of the sun blares out.
Then, from the depth of the horizon the tamed monsters
leap forward. They jump over the meridians. The smoke
and the ocean are like ripped paper hanging from hoops;
they have the same slashes. The beasts roar. The ships sail
past, buck and rear. A whiplash from the lighthouses calms
them down. They return to the docks as to cages, humili-
ated, black.[54]

Although the young traveler had not yet freed himself
from the pleasure of exhausting a metaphor, which the
future poet would know how to merely suggest in a flash,
this description of New York as a circus, for instance, and
many such passages in "Mon voyage à New York" and
"New York in Flashlight," could easily figure among the
other poetic snapshots of *Documentaires*.

Even the paratactic style in Cendrars's inventories of
birds, plants, animals, objects of all kinds, underscores his
perception of the American life principle. His seemingly
artless method of cataloging may seem to result from an
impersonal choice of words picked at random from bro-
chures or even dictionaries. Yet it expresses so appropri-
ately the author's sense of exhilaration at the confronta-
tion with such abundance and variety that Cendrars's
hyperpersonal grasp of what he saw is ever present. Faced
with the multiplicity and the diversity of the American
continent and eager to use language with the same effec-
tiveness, precision, and rapidity as optical instruments
are used, he naturally resorted to simple juxtaposition of
elements perceived. The word that illustrates also ex-
plains. It is not an indirect signifier; it has a pure ontologi-
cal reality that is in total congruence with the poet's
apprehension of the world.

Nevertheless, the verbal photographs have been drawn
from Gustave Lerouge's novel. The poems "Golden

Gate," "Office," "Frisco-City," for instance, reproduce almost word for word entire paragraphs from *Le mystérieux Docteur Cornélius*. "Mushrooming City" is Jorgell City in the novel; the multimillionaire in his office is Mr. Jorgell, one of Lerouge's main heroes; Isidora with her "pigeon-blood" ruby is Jorgell's daughter, and his son Baruch is described by Lerouge as a Brummel youth. The Black Beans Club was also named by Lerouge. Andrée and Frédérique in "Thousand Islands" are two characters from the novel, and the menus are taken verbatim from Lerouge. The list of likenesses could continue endlessly. Do the similarities mean, therefore, that Gustave Lerouge should be credited with Cendrars's poetic empathy of the American continent? Are we faced with a mere hoax? Francis Lacassin's demonstration leaves no doubt. Yet a closer look at the two texts presents a totally different view. Cendrars was not facetiously making fun of all the poetic theories of his time by publishing a literary patchwork in a kind of Dada spirit of rebellion; he was conducting a technical experiment with language. In *L'-Homme foudroyé* he specified that the "trick" was performed to demonstrate to Lerouge that he was a poet (see n. 52). Had the reality conveyed so aptly by Cendrars in these poems already been captured as such by Lerouge? Or was it brought out only through Cendrars's poetic "montage"?

As his earlier life had shown, Cendrars roamed through books as much as through the world. In every city libraries were his haunt. A text was for him what paint and canvas are to a painter. Fascinated by the various levels of significance of language, he performed a transplant operation which lifted a strictly linear prose to the more condensed evocative power of poetry, thus applying to writing a collage technique already common in art. The chunks of prose he reassembled are nothing more than the newspaper cuttings in a Braque painting or the odds and ends that Duchamp raised to the status of an art object. Just as driftwood on a beach can remain in a shapeless heap until a discerning eye picks it out and makes it a work of art, Cendrars saw in Lerouge's prose elements he brought together, ordered, contracted, and chiseled into his vision of the American reality.

As a matter of fact, in the process of "second-degree" writing, Cendrars may unwittingly have been the forerunner of a current trend in the technique of writing. In a recent radio interview, Roland Barthes presented a young writer, Renaud Camus, whose novel *Passage* is built on a multiple framework of references, actual quotations from previous works and passages slightly altered "for the sake of integration" to the author's text. Barthes endorses the modernity of such a "combination of primitive sentences" which shows that "the act of generation of the word and its potential of transformation are substituted for the imitation of pseudoreality."[55] Language, whether in the raw material of independent words or already woven into a previously written text, becomes matter used by the writer just as any object became a ready-made for Marcel Duchamp.

The creative process, then, lies in the angles from which language is highlighted. In *L'Homme foudroyé* Cendrars comments on Lerouge's technique in terms that here take on special significance:

> . . . reject stylization, tell facts, facts, nothing but facts, the largest number of things in the least possible words; and, finally, make an original idea spring forth, stripped of all systems, apart from all associations, perceived from outside as it were, from a hundred angles at the same time and with the help of innumerable telescopes and microscopes, but lit from inside.[56]

As Cendrars derived the verbal material of *Documentaires* from this uncommon storyteller, he undoubtedly did it with the "innumerable telescopes and microscopes" of his mind, "lit from inside" with his own poetic intuition and visual sense. Like an experienced art photographer, Cendrars chose his "mental photographs" in a process of recognition which focuses on the appropriate element, reconstructs, reassembles, and enhances it through an angle of vision not previously perceived.

Thus, whatever the source of his inspiration, Cendrars developed in *Documentaires* a new technique of expression and perception. One could easily apply to his poetry Valéry's statement in his notes to the *Introduction à la méthode de Léonard de Vinci*: "A work of art should always teach us that we have not seen what we see."[57] In these poems the outer eye is seen with an inner eye. All the while aware, with Bachelard, that the object designates us more than we designate the object, Cendrars put to work the advice he offered painters in his articles for the Rose Rouge in 1919, not to seek the reality of the object through a progression in space but reality itself through a progression in depth. His collage technique illustrates clearly the difference between the spatial linear progression of narrative prose and the prismatic volumes in depth of poetry. For example, through the evocation of an old rusty ship, which in Lerouge is described only for the purpose of telling about a shipwreck, Cendrars conjures up the vital core of the city of San Francisco as well, with the drama of its Chinese immigrants; or, starting with the lush beauty of a Canadian spring, he contrasts it with the sudden flare-up of a forest fire, offering his readers not merely a visual narrative experience but stretching the mind to the multidimensional depths of the reality of what he was seeing. In "Office," what reads in Lerouge like strictly technical information takes on a life in which each object is given an individualizing power. With his highly exercised multisensorial perception, Cendrars selected the significant detail that projects the whole and brings to life an entire continent in terse, actively luminous sketches.

Feuilles de route, on the other hand, is the poetic diary of Cendrars's crossings to South America, the "postcards" he sent or intended to send to friends, as he specifies in *Blaise Cendrars vous parle*. Thus the poems achieve the subjective intimacy of his voyage on board the SS *Formosa* and sensitively evoke the people and scenes he saw. In *Feuilles de route*, Cendrars did not set out to write the epic of the sea, as he did for the transsiberian railroad, or to convey an inner vision of a continent through the objective device of verbal photography as in *Documentaires*. He used the personal tone of a postcard, recording the sensual and simple delight of being alive in the marvelous freedom of the ocean, the magnificence of the equator, the boisterous dynamism of this land of the twenty-first century, the solitude of the writer, the characters he met, the city scenes and the seascapes.

In contrast with the harrowing plunge into the divided consciousness of the age which he was dramatizing at the time in his major prose works, Cendrars appears in these poems as a pragmatic idealist, now an epicurean, now a stoic, who responds to all the pleasures of the senses and the mind, savors to the full the ultramarine blue of the sky in the open sea, the scorching sun, the "full moon like another wheel," swimming in the pool on the upper deck, the laughter of his table companions, the white suit he bought in Dakar, the islands where he will never land, "everything pitched in a higher key." Since the first heightening of his senses on his crossing from Libau to New York in 1911, Cendrars always heard the roaring swell of the ocean within him and dreamed of being forever at sea, never landing anywhere. Once he touches land, however, he captures the spirit of a place and its people not only through his uncommon quality of observation, but with the gift of identification with the phenomenon perceived, the art, described later by Bachelard, of seeking out behind visible images the hidden reality of mind as well as of matter.

Although in *Feuilles de route* the personality of the poet is ever present and inescapable, the subjective is conveyed in objectivity. Just as much as North America in *Documentaires*, the life on board a transatlantic liner and in South America are brought to the readers in their immanence. Cendrars shared with his contemporaries the taste for travel and for the evocation of distant lands, which provided a theme for other poets, such as Segalen, Supervielle, Claudel, Michaux, and Morand, in the first quarter of the century. He discarded, however, the lyrical exoticism in vogue in the twenties and did not uphold its aesthetics of diversity. His poems do not read like reports or memoirs of a foreign visitor impressed by the difference, the otherness, of a country. Cendrars lived and wrote with completely transnational consciousness; every part of the world is felt from the inside, made present by his very presence there.

In his effort to capture the organic beat of life through the entire world, Cendrars not only shunned the fashionable exoticism but he also rejected the hermeticism that prevailed in poetry at the time. The postcard technique he inaugurated enabled him to strip poetry of all devices and poeticisms and achieve his goal of writing "without ostentation, simply, true, as one lives,"[58] reaching at times a most difficult simplicity in blending ironic starkness and open candor. The poem "Ocean Letter," from which the English title for the three sequences of *Feuilles de route* is derived, may be seen as a clue to Cendrars's poetic intent in this collection. Under the guise of apparently offhand witty remarks, it conveys the author's conviction that poetry is rooted in life, inner and outer life, and seizes it in direct flashes beyond any probing. From the confinement of his cabin, with only clattering typewriter keys and the laughter of his monkeys for company, to the exaltation of sunrise walks on deck and splashes in the pool, the poet conveys, in "postcard" after "postcard" written along his journey, a world full of things, not registers or conductors of anything, which have nothing to do but exist, organically intact and immediate in his pages. To reflect upon them would be for Cendrars to betray the instantaneous plenitude of being which vibrates through the poetry and gives the effect of life caught untouched, in the transparency of itself.

In the complex web of Cendrars's multitudinous writings these verbal postcards from the Americas certainly seem "tossed off," "done on the side as it were," during his endless rampages among reams of books and in innumerable countries. In their totality they constitute a landmark in the modern renewal of sequential poetry, and although, in the age of supersonic speed and jet flights, they evoke a bygone era of leisurely travels, they act upon the reader of today and tomorrow through the seizure of a world into which, all his senses and his mind alert, a poet plunges: "Excentric. In total solitude. In anonymous communion. With all that is root and crowning top and that throbs, enjoys, and is entranced. Manifestations of this congenital hallucination that life is in all its forms and the continuous activity of consciousness."[59]

Notes to Introduction

All material quoted from Cendrars's works is taken from *Oeuvres complètes de Blaise Cendrars* (Paris: Club Français du livre, 1968-1971) and from *Inédits Secrets* (Paris: Club Français de Livre, 1969). The abbreviations *O.C.* and *I.S.* used in the notes refer, respectively, to these two sources. All translations are my own.

1. Henry Miller, "Blaise Cendrars, Salute from Afar," MS of article sent to *Gazette de Lausanne*, March 11, 1960, Henry Miller Collection, Research Library, University of California, Los Angeles. Published in the *Gazette de Lausanne*, no. 23 (January 28-29, 1961).

2. Henry Miller, "Tribute to Blaise Cendrars," in *The Wisdom of the Heart* (New York: New Directions), 1941, p. 152.

3. Jean Buhler, *Blaise Cendrars, homme libre, poète au coeur du monde* (Bienne, Switzerland: Éditions du Panorama, 1960), p. 106.

4. Chapter title in John Dos Passos, *Orient Express* (New York: Jonathan Cape and Harrison Smith, 1930).

5. Ferreira de Castro, "L'écrivain et l'homme Cendrars," *Mercure de France* (May 1962), p. 39.

6. *Le Panama ou les Aventures de mes sept oncles*, in *O.C.*, I, 38.

7. *I.S.*, p. 29.

8. The article on Rémy de Gourmont, entitled "Le dernier des justes," was published by Cendrars in *Les Hommes Nouveaux* (1913).

9. *O.C.*, VI, 140.

10. *L'Homme foudroyé*, in *O.C.*, IX, 45.

11. *I.S.*, pp. 212-233.

12. *Blaise Cendrars vous parle*, in *O.C.*, XIII, 156-159.

13. *Aujourd'hui*, in *O.C.*, VI, 55-56.

14. *Ibid.*, p. 51.

15. Cendrars himself has repeatedly refused to express any opinion on the matter, and it seems superfluous here to raise again an issue that in no way adds to or detracts from the undeniable renewal brought to twentieth-century poetry by Blaise Cendrars. The interested reader may consult the works of Jacques-Henry Lévesque, Louis Parrot, and Marc Poupon listed in the bibliography, as well as M. J. Durry's *Guillaume Apollinaire Alcools* (Paris: Socíeté d'Etudes et d'Enseignement Supérieur, 1956), pp. 234-301.

16. *Prose du Transsibérien*, in *O.C.*, I, 28.

17. *I.S.*, pp. 356-363.

18. *Ibid.*, p. 360.

19. *L'année 1913: Les formes esthétiques de l'oeuvre d'art à la veille*

de la première guerre mondiale, collective study directed by Liliane Brion Guerry (Paris: Klinsieck, 1971).

20. "Orion," *Feuilles de route,* in *O.C.,* I, 173; *Ocean Letters,* p. 155, below.

21. Philippe Soupault, "Enfin Cendrars vint," *Mercure de France* (May 1962), p. 87.

22. *J'ai tué,* in *Aujourd'hui,* in *O.C.,* VI, 12.

23. Although these works did not appear in book form until 1919 and 1926, excerpts from *La fin du monde filmée par l'ange Notre-Dame* appeared in *La Caravane* in October 1916 and in *Mercure de France* in December 1918. Copies of the manuscript of *L'Eubage* were deposited at Éditions de la Sirène as early as May 1918.

24. The term "postmodern" is used here in the sense given to it by Ihab Hassan, "POSTmodernISM," *New Literary History,* III, no. 1 (Autumn 1971).

25. Fernand Léger, "Réponse à une enquête de René Clair," *Europe,* special issue on Fernand Léger, no. 508-509 (August-September 1971).

26. *Trop c'est trop,* in *O.C.,* XV, 102-103.

27. *L'Homme foudroyé,* in *O.C.,* IX, 330.

28. *Aujourd'hui,* in *O.C.,* VI, 71.

29. Aracy A. Amaral, *Blaise Cendrars no Brasil e os modernistos* (São Paulo: Martins Press, 1970), p. 41.

30. *Aujourd'hui,* in *O.C.,* VI, 14.

31. Amaral, *Blaise Cendrars,* pp. 41 n. 29, 155-161.

32. *Dan Yack,* in *O.C.,* V, 53.

33. Robert Scholes, *Structuralism in Literature* (New Haven: Yale University Press, 1974), p. 169-200.

34. *Une nuit dans la forêt,* in *O.C.,* VI, 142.

35. *Ibid.,* p. 138.

36. Henry Miller, "Tribute to Blaise Cendrars," in *The Wisdom of the Heart,* p. 152.

37. *Une nuit dans la forêt,* in *O.C.,* VI, 139.

38. *Hollywood: La Mecque du cinéma,* in *O.C.,* VII, 132.

39. *L'Homme foudroyé,* in *O.C.,* IX, 45.

40. *Bourlinguer,* in *O.C.,* XI, 116.

41. In his introduction to Blaise Cendrars's poems, Jacques-Henry Lévesque explains at length the esoteric meaning of the phrase chosen intuitively by Cendrars as the title of the complete edition of his poems (*Poésies complètes de Blaise Cendrars* [Paris: Denoël, 1944], p. 41 n. 1).

42. *Bourlinguer,* in *O.C.,* XI, 167.

43. Raymond Dumay, "Blaise Savonarole à Paris," in *O.C.,* XIV, V.

45. "Bourlingueur des mers du Sud," in *O.C.*, XIV, 318.

46. Walter Albert, introduction to *Selected Writings of Blaise Cendrars* (New York: New Directions, 1966), pp. 24, 28.

47. Paul Morand, preface to *Du Monde Entier* (Paris: Gallimard, 1967), p. 11.

48. Charles Albert Cingria, *La civilisation de Saint-Gall*, in *Oeuvres complètes*, II (Lausanne: Éditions de l'Age d'Homme, 1967), 219-220.

49. Fernand Léger, *Functions of Painting*, Documents of Twentieth Century Art, trans. Alexandra Anderson (New York: Viking Press, 1973), p. 35. Originally published in *Bulletin de l'Effort Moderne* (Paris, 1924).

50. "Contrastes," *Dix-neuf poèmes élastiques*, in *O.C.*, I, 60.

51. *L'Homme foudroyé*, in *O.C.*, IX, 191.

52. *Ibid.*, pp. 204-209.

53. Francis Lacassin, "Quand la poésie copie le feuilleton," *Magazine Littéraire*, no. 9 (July-August 1967); Francis Lacassin, *Les poèmes du Docteur Cornélius par Blaise Cendrars et Gustave Lerouge* (Paris: Martineau, n.d.).

54. "New York in Flashlight," in *I.S.*, p. 241.

55. "Roland Barthes interroge Renaud Camus," *La Quinzaine Littéraire* (May 1-15, 1975), pp. 8, 9.

56. *L'Homme foudroyé*, in *O.C.*, IX, 198.

57. Paul Valéry, *Oeuvres*, I (Paris: Éditions de la Nouvelle Revue Française, 1957), 1165.

58. *Trop c'est trop*, in *O.C.*, XV, 24.

59. *Aujourd'hui*, in *O.C.*, VI, 6.

Modigliani's drawing of Cendrars, 1917 (from *Dix-neuf poèmes élastiques*). [Copyright Association pour la diffusion des arts graphiques et plastiques (ADAGP)]

DOCUMENTAIRES

DOCUMENTARIES

WEST

I. ROOF-GARDEN

Pendant des semaines les ascenseurs ont hissé hissé des
   caisses des caisses de terre végétale
Enfin
A force d'argent et de patience
Des bosquets s'épanouissent
Des pelouses d'un vert tendre
Une source vive jaillit entre les rhododendrons et les
   camélias
Au sommet de l'édifice l'édifice de briques et d'acier
Le soir
Les waiters graves comme des diplomates vêtus de
   blanc se penchent sur le gouffre de la ville
Et les massifs s'éclairent d'un million de petite lampes
   versicolores
Je crois Madame murmura le jeune homme d'une voix
   vibrante de passion contenue
Je crois que nous serons admirablement ici
Et d'un large geste il montrait la large mer
Le va-et-vient
Les fanaux des navires géants
La géante statue de la Liberté
Et l'énorme panorama de la ville coupée de ténèbres
   perpendiculaires et de lumières crues

WEST*

I. ROOF-GARDEN

Week after week the elevators have hoisted
   hoisted up crates and crates of loam
Finally
Through much money and patience
Groves blossom out
Lawns of a soft green shade
A living spring gushes forth between the
   rhododendrons and the camellias
At the top of the building the brick and steel
   building
In the evening
Waiters solemn like diplomats dressed in white
   lean over the abyss of the city
And a million versicolor little lamps light up the
   shrubbery
I believe Madam the young man murmured in a
   voice quivering with restrained passion
I believe we will do admirably here
And with a wide gesture he pointed to the wide sea
The hustle and bustle
The sidelights of the gigantic vessels
The gigantic Statue of Liberty
And the vast panorama of the town streaked
   with perpendicular shades and garish lights

*An asterisk indicates an annotation by the translator. See "Notes on the Poems," pp. 242-245.

Le vieux savant et les deux milliardaires sont seuls sur
   la terrasse
Magnifique jardin
Massifs de fleurs
Ciel étoilé
Les trois vieillards demeurent silencieux prêtent l'oreille
   au bruit des rires et des voix joyeuses qui montent
   des fenêtres illuminées
Et à la chanson murmurée de la mer qui s'enchaîne au
   gramophone

II. SUR L'HUDSON

Le canot électrique glisse sans bruit entre les nombreux
   navires ancrés dans l'immense estuaire et qui battent
   pavillon de toutes les nations du monde
Les grands clippers chargés de bois et venus du Canada
   ferlaient leurs voiles géantes
Les paquebots de fer lançaient des torrents de fumée
   noire
Un peuple de dockers appartenant à toutes les races du
   globe s'affairait dans le tapage des sirènes à vapeur
   et les sifflets des usines et des trains
L'élégante embarcation est entièrement en bois de teck
Au centre se dresse une sorte de cabine assez semblable
   à celle des gondoles vénitiennes

III. AMPHITRYON

Après le dîner servi dans les jardins d'hiver au milieu
   des massifs de citronniers de jasmins d'orchidées
Il y a bal sur la pelouse du parc illuminé
Mais la principale attraction sont les cadeaux envoyés
   à Miss Isadora
On remarque surtout un rubis « sang de pigeon » dont
   la grosseur et l'éclat sont incomparables
Aucune des jeunes filles présentes n'en possède un qui
   puisse lui être comparé

The old scientist and the two multimillionaires are
   alone on the terrace
Magnificent garden
Flower beds
Starred sky
The three old men remain silent listening to
   the peals of laughter and merry voices rising
   from the lighted windows
And to the murmured song of the sea which tunes in
   with the record player

II. ON THE HUDSON

The electric motorboat glides silently between the
   many vessels that lie at anchor in the broad
   estuary and fly the flags of all the nations of the
   world
The large lumber-laden clippers that sailed from
   Canada furled their gigantic sails
The iron liners were belching out torrents of black
   smoke
A multitude of dockhands belonging to all races of
   the globe bustled about in the din of blasts from
   steam foghorns and tooting factories and trains
The elegant craft is made entirely of teakwood
In the middle rises a kind of cabin rather like the
   one on Venetian gondolas

III. AMPHITRYON

After the dinner served in the winter gardens among clusters
   of lemon trees jasmine and orchids
There is a dance on the illuminated park lawn
But the main attraction is the presents sent to Miss Isadora
A pigeon-blood ruby of incomparable size and glitter
   is particularly noticed
None of the young ladies there owns one that compares
   with it

Élégamment vêtus
D'habiles détectives mêlés à la foule des invités veillent
   sur cette gemme et la protègent.

IV. OFFICE

Radiateurs et ventilateurs à air liquide
Douze téléphones et cinq postes de T.S.F.
D'admirables classeurs électriques contiennent les
   myriades de dossiers industriels et scientifiques sur
   les affaires les plus variées
Le milliardaire ne se sent vraiment chez lui que dans
   ce cabinet de travail
Les larges verrières donnent sur le parc et la ville
Le soir les lampes à vapeur de mercure y répandent
   une douce lueur azurée
C'est de là que partent les ordres de vente et d'achat
   qui culbutent parfois les cours de Bourse dans le
   monde entier

V. JEUNE FILLE

Légère robe en crêpe de Chine
La jeune fille
Élégance et richesse
Cheveux d'un blond fauve où brille un rang de perles
Physionomie régulière et calme qui reflète la franchise
   et la bonté
Ses grands yeux d'un bleu de mer presque vert sont
   clairs et hardis
Elle a ce teint frais et velouté d'une roseur spéciale qui
   semble l'apanage des jeunes filles américaines

VI. JEUNE HOMME

C'est le Brummel de la Fifth Avenue
Cravate en toile d'or semée de fleurettes de diamants

Elegantly dressed
Shrewd detectives mingling with the crowd
  of guests watch over this gem and protect it

IV. OFFICE

Liquid-air ventilators and radiators
Twelve telephones and five radio sets
Admirable electric file cabinets contain the myriads of
  industrial and scientific documents on the most varied
  items of business
The multimillionaire feels really at home only in this office
The wide plate-glass windows look out on the park
  and the city
In the evening the vapor lamps cast a soft azured light
  over them
There sale and purchase orders are issued which sometimes
  knock the bottom out of the stock market all over
  the world

V. YOUNG GIRL

Light dress in crepe de Chine
The young girl
Elegance and wealth
A row of pearls sparkling in tawny blond hair
Candor and kindness on a regular and calm countenance
Her large blue eyes of an almost green sea blue
  are clear and daring
She has that fresh velvety complexion of a particular pink
  which seems to belong to young American girls

VI. YOUNG MAN

It is Brummel on Fifth Avenue
Gold linen tie spangled with tiny diamond flowers

Complet en étoffe métallique rose et violet
Bottine en véritable peau de requin et dont chaque
   bouton est une petite perle noire
Il exhibe un pyjama en flanelle d'amiante un autre complet
   en étoffe de verre un gilet en peau de crocodile
Son valet de chambre savonne ses pièces d'or
Il n'a jamais en portefeuille que des banknotes neuves
   et parfumées

VII. TRAVAIL

Des malfaiteurs viennent de faire sauter le pont de
   l'estacade
Les wagons ont pris feu au fond de la vallée
Des blessés nagent dans l'eau bouillante que lâche la
   locomotive éventrée
Des torches vivantes courent parmi les décombres et les
   jets de vapeur
D'autres wagons sont restés suspendus à 60 mètres de
   hauteur
Des hommes armés de torches électriques et à l'acé-
   tylène descendent le sentier de la vallée
Et les secours s'organisent avec une silencieuse rapidité
Sous le couvert des joncs des roseaux des saules les
   oiseaux aquatiques font un joli remue-ménage
L'aube tarde à venir
Que déjà une équipe de cent charpentiers appelés par
   télégraphe et venus par train spécial s'occupent à
   reconstruire le pont
Pan pan-pan
Passe-moi les clous

VIII. TRESTLE-WORK

Rencontre-t-on un cours d'eau ou une vallée profonde
On la passe sur un pont de bois en attendant que les
   recettes de la compagnie permettent d'en construire
   un en pierre ou en fer

Pink and purple suit in metallic cloth
Genuine sharkskin boots on which every button
   is a small black pearl
He sports a pair of asbestos flannel pajamas another suit
   in glass twill a crocodile-skin vest
His valet washes his gold coins in soap and water
He never has anything in his purse but new scented
   bank notes

VII. WORK

Racketeers have just blown up the bridge on the
   elevated runway
Carriages have caught fire at the bottom of the valley
The wounded are weltering in the scalding hot water
   spouting out of the smashed engine
Living torches run through the debris and the steam jets
Other carriages are left hanging 200 feet high
Men armed with electric and acetylene torches walk down
   the path of the valley
And help is organized with silent speed
In the shelter of rushes reeds and willows the aquatic birds
   are all in a flutter
Dawn tarries*
That already a team of a hundred carpenters called in by
   telegram and brought by special train are busy with the
   reconstruction of the bridge
Bang Bang Bang
Hand me the nails

VIII. TRESTLE-WORK

Should you come upon a waterway or a deep valley
You will cross it on a wooden bridge until the company's
   profits allow it to build a stone or an iron one

Les charpentiers américains n'ont pas de rivaux dans
  l'art de construire ces ponts
On commence par poser un lit de pierres dures
Puis on dresse un premier chevalet
Lequel en supporte un second puis un troisième puis
  un quatrième
Autant qu'il en faut pour atteindre le niveau de la rive
Sur le dernier chevalet deux poutres
Sur les deux poutres deux rails
Ces constructions audacieuses ne sont renforcées ni
  par des croix de St. André ni par des fers en T
Elles ne tiennent que par quelques poutrelles et quelques
  chevilles qui maintiennent l'écartement des chevalets
Et c'est un tout
C'est un pont
C'est un beau pont

IX. LES MILLE ILES

En cet endroit le paysage est un des plus beaux qui se
  trouvent en Amérique du Nord
La nappe immense du lac est d'un bleu presque blanc
Des centaines et des centaines de petites îles verdoyantes
  flottent sur la calme surface des eaux limpides
Les délicieux cottages construits en briques de couleurs
  vives donnent à ce paysage l'aspect d'un royaume
  enchanté
Des luxueux canots d'érable d'acajou élégamment
  pavoisés et couverts de tentes multicolores vont et
  viennent d'une île à l'autre
Toute idée de fatigue de labeur de misère est absente
  de ce décor gracieux pour milliardaires

Le soleil disparaît à l'horizon du lac Ontario
Les nuages baignent leurs plis dans des cuves de pourpre
  violette d'écarlate et d'orangé
Quel beau soir murmurent Andrée et Frédérique assises
  sur la terrasse d'un château du moyen âge
Et les dix mille canots moteurs répondent à leur extase

American carpenters are unrivaled in the art of building
    these bridges
First a bed of hard stones is laid down
Then a first trestle is set up
On which stands a second a third then a fourth
As many as necessary to reach the level of the bank
On the last trestle two beams
On the two beams two rails
Neither counterbraces nor **T** irons reinforce these daring
    constructions
Only a few girders and pegs which keep the trestles properly
    spaced hold them together
And it is a totality
It is a bridge
It is a beautiful bridge

IX. THOUSAND ISLANDS

Here the landscape is one of the most beautiful in
    North America
The immense sheet of the lake is of an almost white
    blue shade
Hundreds and hundreds of small green islands float on the
    calm surface of the limpid waters
The delightful cottages built in brightly colored bricks
    make that landscape look like an enchanted kingdom
Luxurious maple or mahogany boats dressed with elegant
    signal flags and bunting and covered with multicolored
    canopies ply between the islands
All idea of strain toil and poverty is alien to this graceful
    setting for multimillionaires

The sun disappears on the horizon of Lake Ontario
The clouds dip their folds into vats in dyes of violet-purple
    scarlet and orange
What a beautiful evening whisper Andrée and Frédérique
    sitting on the terrace of a medieval castle
And the drone of ten thousand motorboats answers
    their ecstasy

X. LABORATOIRE

Visite des serres
Le thermo-siphon y maintient une température cons-
    tante
La terre est saturée d'acide formique de manganèse
    et d'autres substances qui impriment à la végétation
    une puissance formidable
D'un jour à l'autre les feuilles poussent les fleurs éclosent
    les fruits mûrissent
Les racines grâce à un dispositif ingénieux baignent
    dans un courant électrique qui assure cette croissance
    monstrueuse
Les canons paragrêle détruisent nimbus et cumulus
Nous rentrons en ville en traversant les landes
La matinée est radieuse
Les bruyères d'une sombre couleur de pourpre et les
    genêts d'or ne sont pas encore défleuris
Les goélands et les mauves tracent de grands cercles
    dans le bleu léger du ciel

FAR-WEST

I. CUCUMINGO

L'hacienda de San-Bernardino
Elle est bâtie au centre d'une verdoyante vallée arrosée
    par une multitude de petits ruisseaux venus des mon-
    tagnes circonvoisines
Les toits sont de tuiles rouges sous les ombrages des
    sycomores et des lauriers

Les truites pullulent dans les ruisseaux
D'innombrables troupeaux paissent en liberté dans les
    grasses prairies
Les vergers regorgent de fruits poires pommes raisins
    ananas figues oranges

X. LABORATORY

Visit to the greenhouse
The thermosiphon maintains a constant temperature
The soil is saturated with formic acid and permanganate and
    other substances that infuse the vegetation with
    tremendous strength
Leaves grow flowers blossom out fruit ripens overnight
Owing to an ingenious device roots bathe in an electric
    current which guarantees that monstrous growth
The antihail cannons smash the clouds nimbus and cumulus
We cross the moors to return to town
It is a bright morning
The dark purple heather and the golden furze
    have not yet lost their blossom
The sea gulls and kittiwakes circle widely in the light azure
    of the sky

FAR-WEST

I. CUCUMINGO

The San Bernardino hacienda
It is built in the middle of a green valley
    watered by innumerable small streams
    that flow from the surrounding mountains
The roofs covered with red tiles are shaded by sycamores
    and oleanders

The streams are teeming with trout
Countless herds graze freely in the lush meadows
The orchards are heavy with fruit pears apples grapes
    pineapples figs oranges

Et dans les potagers
Les légumes du vieux monde poussent à côté de ceux
    des contrées tropicales

Le gibier abonde dans le canton
Le colin de Californie
Le lapin à queue de coton *cottontail*
Le lièvre aux longues oreilles *jackass*
La caille la tourterelle la perdrix
Le canard et l'oie sauvages
L'antilope
Il est vrai qu'on y rencontre encore le chat sauvage et
    le serpent à sonnettes *rattlesnake*
Mais il n'y a plus de puma aujourd'hui

II. DORYPHA

Les jours de fête
Quand les indiens et les vaqueros s'enivrent de whisky et
    de pulque
Dorypha danse
Au son de la guitare mexicaine
Habaneras si entraînantes
Qu'on vient de plusieurs lieues pour l'admirer

Aucune femme ne sait aussi bien qu'elle
Draper la mantille de soie
Et parer sa chevelure blonde
D'un ruban
D'un peigne
D'une fleur

III. L'OISEAU-MOQUEUR

La chaleur est accablante
Balcon ombragé de jasmin de Virginie et de chèvre-
    feuille pourpré
Dans le grand silence de la campagne sommeillante
On discerne

And in the vegetable gardens
Old World vegetables grow next to those from tropical lands

Game abounds in the county
The California bobwhite
The cottontail rabbit
The long-eared jackrabbit*
The quail the turtledove the partridge
The wild duck and goose
The antelope
You can still come across the wildcat
    and the rattlesnake there
But there are no more pumas today

II. DORYPHA

On fiesta days
When the Indians and the vaqueros get drunk on whiskey
    and pulque
Dorypha dances
To the rhythm of the Mexican guitar
Such spirited habaneras
That people come from miles away to admire her

No woman knows better
How to wrap the silk mantilla around herself
And adorn her blond hair
With a ribbon
A comb
A flower

III. THE MOCKINGBIRD

Sweltering heat
A balcony shaded with trumpet creeper and purple
    honeysuckle
In the deep silence of the slumbering countryside
You can hear

Le glou-glou des petits torrents
Le mugissement lointain des grands troupeaux de
bœufs dans les pâturages
Le chant du rossignol
Le sifflement cristallin des crapauds géants
Le hululement des rapaces nocturnes
Et le cri de l'oiseau-moqueur dans les cactus

IV. VILLE-CHAMPIGNON

Vers la fin de l'année 1911 un groupe de financiers
yankees décide la fondation d'une ville en plein Far-
West au pied des Montagnes Rocheuses
Un mois ne s'est pas écoulé que la nouvelle cité encore
sans aucune maison est déjà reliée par trois lignes
au réseau ferré de l'Union
Les travailleurs accourent de toutes parts
Dès le deuxième mois trois églises sont édifiées et
cinq théâtres en pleine exploitation
Autour d'une place où subsistent quelques beaux
arbres une forêt de poutres métalliques bruit nuit et
jour de la cadence des marteaux
Treuils
Halètement des machines
Les carcasses d'acier des maisons de trente étages
commencent à s'aligner
Des parois de briques souvent de simples plaques
d'aluminium bouchent les interstices de la charpente
de fer
On coule en quelques heures des édifices en béton armé
selon le procédé Edison
Par une sorte de superstition on ne sait comment baptiser
la ville et un concours est ouvert avec une tombola
et des prix par le plus grand journal de la ville qui
cherche également un nom

The gurgling of small rushing streams
The distant lowing of large herds of cattle
  in the pastures
The song of the nightingale
The crystal-clear hissing of gigantic toads
Screeching nocturnal birds of prey
And the mockingbird chirping in the cacti

IV. MUSHROOMING CITY

Toward the end of the year 1911 a group of Yankee financiers
  decides to build a city in the heart of the Far-West
  at the foot of the Rockies
A month has hardly gone by and three lines already connect
  the still houseless city to the railway network
  of the Union
Workmen come in droves from all over
By the second month three churches have been erected
  and five theaters are in business
Around a square where a few beautiful trees are still standing
  a forest of metallic beams rustles night and day
  to the stroke of the hammer
Winches
Panting machinery
The steel frames of the thirty-storied houses start
  to fall into line
Brick walls often mere aluminum panels fill in
  the gaps in the iron frames
Within a few hours reinforced concrete buildings are
  cast according to the Edison process
A certain kind of superstition keeps people from giving a
  name to the city and a competition with a lottery and
  prizes is opened by the biggest newspaper in town which
  is also in search of a name

V. CLUB

La rue bien qu'indiquée sur le plan offlciel de la ville
n'est encore constituée que par des clôtures de
planches et des monceaux de gravats
On ne la franchit qu'en sautant au petit bonheur les
flaques d'eau et les fondrières
Au bout du boulevard inachevé qu'éclairent de puissantes
lampes à arc est le club des Haricots Noirs qui est
aussi une agence matrimoniale
Coiffés d'un feutre de cow-boy ou d'une casquette à
oreillettes
Le visage dur
Des hommes descendent de leur 60 chevaux qu'ils
étrennent s'inscrivent consultent l'album des photo-
graphies
Choisissent leur fiancée qui sur un câble s'embarquera
à Cherbourg sur le *Kaiser Wilhelm* et arrivera à
toute vapeur
Ce sont surtout des Allemandes
Un lad vêtu de noir chaussé de molleton d'une correction
glaciale ouvre la porte et toise le nouveau venu d'un
air soupçonneux
Je bois un cocktail au whisky puis un deuxième puis un
troisième
Puis un mint-julep un milk-mother un prairy-oyster
un night-cap

VI. SQUAW-WIGWAM

Quand on a franchi la porte vermoulue faite de planches
arrachées à des caisses d'emballage et à laquelle des
morceaux de cuir servent de gonds
On se trouve dans une salle basse
Enfumée
Odeur de poisson pourri
Relents de graisse rance avec affectation

Panoplies barbares
Couronnes de plumes d'aigle colliers de dents de puma
ou de griffes d'ours

V. CLUB

Although the street is marked on the official map
   there is nothing yet but board fences and heaps
   of rubbish
It can be crossed haphazardly only by jumping over puddles
   and slushy potholes
At the end of the unfinished boulevard lit by powerful
   arc lamps stands the Black Beans Club which is also
   a marriage agency
Wearing felt cowboy hats or caps with earflaps
Tough-looking
Men get off the sixty horses they are riding for the
   first time register study the photograph album
Choose their brides who sent for by cable will board
   the *Kaiser Wilhelm* in Cherbourg and arrive
   full steam ahead
These are mostly German girls
A stableboy in black wearing swanskin shoes glacially
   correct opens the door and sizes up the newcomer
   suspiciously
I have a whiskey cocktail then a second then a third
Then a mint-julep a milk-mother a prairy-oyster
   a night-cap

VI. SQUAW-WIGWAM

After passing through the worm-eaten door made of boards
   that have been knocked off crates and hinged with
   leather straps
You are in a low room
Filled with smoke
Stench of rotten fish
Self-conceited reeks of rancid fat

Barbaric panoplies
Eagle-feather crowns puma-teeth or bear-claw necklaces

Arcs flèches tomahawks
Mocassins
Bracelets de graines et de verroteries
On voit encore
Des couteaux à scalper une ou deux carabines d'ancien
modèle un pistolet à pierre des bois d'élan et de renne
et toute une collection de petits sacs brodés pour
mettre le tabac
Plus trois calumets très anciens formés d'une pierre
tendre emmanchée d'un roseau

Éternellement penchée sur le foyer
La centenaire propriétaire de cet établissement se
conserve comme un jambon et s'enfume et se couenne
et se boucane comme sa pipe centenaire et le noir
de sa bouche et le trou noir de son œil

VII. VILLE-DE-FRISCO

C'est une antique carcasse dévorée par la rouille
Vingt fois réparée la machine ne donne pas plus de 7 à
8 nœuds à l'heure
D'ailleurs par économie on ne brûle que des escarbilles
et des déchets de charbon
On hisse des voiles de fortune chaque fois que le vent
est favorable
Avec sa face écarlate ses sourcils touffus son nez bour-
geonnant master Hopkins est un véritable marin
Des petits anneaux d'argent percent ses oreilles
Ce navire est exclusivement chargé de cercueils de
Chinois décédés en Amérique et qui ont désiré se
faire enterrer dans la terre natale
Caisses oblongues coloriées de rouge ou de bleu clair
ou couvertes d'inscriptions dorées
C'est là un genre de marchandise qu'il est interdit de
transporter

Bows arrows tomahawks
Moccasins
Seed and glass-bead bracelets
One can still see
Scalping knives one or two old-fashioned rifles
    a flint pistol elk and reindeer antlers and
    a whole array of small embroidered tobacco
    pouches
Plus three very ancient peace pipes made of a soft
    stone fitted to a reed

Forever stooping over the hearth
The hundred-year-old mistress of the place
    is preserved like a ham smoke-dries herself
    cures her pig's skin chars herself like her
    century-old pipe and the black in her mouth
    and the black hole of her eye*

VII. FRISCO-CITY

It is an antique carcass eaten up by rust
The engine repaired twenty times does not make
    more than 7 to 8 knots
Besides to save expense cinders and coal waste
    are its only fuel
Makeshift sails are hoisted whenever there is
    a fair wind*
With his ruddy face his bushy eyebrows his pimply nose
    Master Hopkins is a true sailor
Small silver rings hang from his pierced ears
The ship's cargo is exclusively coffins of Chinese
    who died in America and wished to be buried
    in their homeland
Oblong boxes painted red or light blue or covered
    with golden characters
Just the type of merchandise it is illegal to ship

VIII. VANCOUVER

Dix heures du soir viennent de sonner à peine distinctes
    dans l'épais brouillard qui ouate les docks et les
    navires du port
Les quais sont déserts et la ville livrée au sommeil
On longe une côte basse et sablonneuse où souffle un
    vent glacial et où viennent déferler les longues lames
    du Pacifique
Cette tache blafarde dans les ténèbres humides c'est
    la gare du Canadian du Grand Tronc
Et ces halos bleuâtres dans le vent sont les paquebots
    en partance pour le Klondyke le Japon et les grandes
    Indes
Il fait si noir que je puis à peine déchiffrer les inscriptions
    des rues où je cherche avec une lourde valise un
    hôtel bon marché

Tout le monde est embarqué
Les rameurs se courbent sur leurs avirons et la lourde
    embarcation chargée jusqu'au bordage pousse entre
    les hautes vagues
Un petit bossu corrige de temps en temps la direction
    d'un coup de barre
Se guidant dans le brouillard sur les appels d'une sirène
On se cogne contre la masse sombre du navire et par
    la hanche tribord grimpent des chiens samoyèdes
Filasses dans le gris-blanc-jaune
Comme si l'on chargeait du brouillard

TERRES ALÉOUTIENNES

I

Hautes falaises contre les vents glacés du pôle
Au centre de fertiles prairies
Rennes élans bœufs musqués

VIII. VANCOUVER

Ten P.M. has just struck barely heard through the thick fog
    that mufflles the docks and the ships in the harbor
The wharfs are deserted and the town is wrapped in sleep
You stroll along a low sandy shore swept by an icy wind
    and the long billows of the Pacific
That lurid spot in the dank darkness is the station of the
    Canadian Grand Trunk
And those bluish patches in the wind are the liners
    bound for the Klondike Japan and the West Indies
It is so dark that I can hardly make out the signs
    in the streets where lugging a heavy suitcase
    I am looking for a cheap hotel

Everyone is on board
The oarsmen are bent on their oars and the heavy craft
    loaded to the brim plows through the high waves
A small hunchback at the helm checks the tiller
    now and then
Adjusting his steering through the fog to the calls
    of a foghorn
We bump against the dark bulk of the ship and on the
    starboard quarter Samoyed dogs are climbing up
Flaxen in the gray-white-yellow
As if fog was being taken in freight

ALEUTIAN ISLANDS

I

High cliffs lashed by icy polar winds
In the center lush meadows
Reindeer elks musk-oxen

Les renards bleus les castors
Ruisseaux poissonneux
Une plage basse a été aménagée pour l'élevage des
    phoques à fourrure
Sur le sommet de la falaise on recueille les nids de
    l'eider dont les plumes constituent une véritable
    richesse

II

Vastes et solides bâtiments qui abritent un nombre assez
    considérable de trafiquants
Tout autour d'un petit jardin où l'on a réuni tous les
    végétaux capables de résister aux rigueurs du climat
Sorbiers pins saules arctiques
Plates-bandes de bruyères et de plantes alpestres

III

Baie parsemée d'îlots rocheux
Par groupes de cinq ou six les phoques se chauffent au
    soleil
Ou étendus sur le sable
Ils jouent entre eux avec cette espèce de cri guttural qui
    ressemble à un aboiement
A côté de la hutte des Esquimaux il y a un hangar pour
    la préparation des peaux

FLEUVE

MISSISSIPI

A cet endroit le fleuve est presque aussi large qu'un lac
Il roule des eaux jaunâtres et boueuses entre deux berges
    marécageuses
Plantes aquatiques que continuent les acréages des
    cotonniers
Çà et là apparaissent les villes et les villages tapis au fond

The Arctic foxes the beavers
Brooks swarming with fish
A low beach has been prepared to breed fur seals
On top of the cliff are collected the eider's nests
Its feathers are worth a real fortune

II

Large and sturdy buildings which shelter a
    considerable number of traders
All around a small garden where all vegetation
    able to withstand the severe climate has
    been brought together
Mountain ash pine trees Arctic willows
Beds of heather and Alpine plants

III

Bay spiked with rocky islets
In groups of five or six the seals bask in the sun
Or stretching out on the sand
They play together howling in that kind of hoarse tone
    that sounds like a dog's bark
Next to the Eskimos' hut is a shed where
    the skins are treated

RIVER

MISSISSIPPI

Here the river is almost as wide as a lake
It rolls yellowish muddy waters between two
    marshy banks
Aquatic plants merge into acres of cotton trees
Here and there appear towns and villages nestling

de quelque petite baie avec leurs usines avec leurs
hautes cheminées noires avec leurs longues estacades
qui s'avancent leurs longues estacades sur pilotis
qui s'avancent bien avant dans l'eau

Chaleur accablante
La cloche du bord sonne pour le lunch
Les passagers arborent des complets à carreaux des
cravates hurlantes des gilets rutilants comme les
cocktails incendiaires et les sauces corrosives

On aperçoit beaucoup de crocodiles
Les jeunes alertes et frétillants
Les gros le dos recouvert d'une mousse verdâtre se
laissent aller à la dérive

La végétation luxuriante annonce l'approche de la zone
tropicale
Bambous géants palmiers tulipiers lauriers cèdres
Le fleuve lui-même a doublé de largeur
Il est tout parsemé d'îlots flottants d'où l'approche du
bateau fait s'élever des nuées d'oiseaux aquatiques
Steam-boats voiliers chalands embarcations de toutes
sortes et d'immenses trains de bois
Une vapeur jaune monte des eaux surchauffées du
fleuve

C'est par centaines maintenant que les crocos s'ébattent
autour de nous
On entend le claquement sec de leurs mâchoires et l'on
distingue très bien leur petit œil féroce
Les passagers s'amusent à leur tirer dessus avec des
carabines de précison
Quand un tireur émérite réussit ce tour de force de tuer
ou de blesser une bête à mort
Ses congénères se précipitent sur elle la déchirent
Férocement
Avec des petits cris assez semblables au vagissement
d'un nouveau-né

far back in some small bay with their factories
with their tall black chimneys with their long
piers jutting out their long piers on piles
well out into the water

Crushing heat
The lunch bell rings on board
The passengers sport checked suits garish ties
    blazing vests like the fiery cocktails
    and the corrosive sauces

You can see many crocodiles
The young brisk and frisky
The bigger ones with their greenish mossy backs
    float adrift

The lush vegetation announces the nearby
    tropical zone
Gigantic bamboos palm trees tulip trees oleanders cedars
The river itself is now twice as wide
It is strewn all over with floating islets from which
    clouds of aquatic birds whirl away as the ship
    draws near
Steamboats sailboats barges craft of all kinds
    and huge rafts of logs
A yellow haze rises above the overheated waters of the
    river

Now the crocs bound and leap about by the hundreds
    around us
You can hear the sharp snap of their jaws and see
    very clearly their small fierce eyes
The passengers' entertainment is to shoot at them
    with precision rifles
When a crack shot manages to kill or wound an animal
    to death
Its fellows rush to it tear it apart
Ferociously
Squealing rather like a wailing newborn babe

LE SUD

I. TAMPA

Le train vient de faire halte
Deux voyageurs seulement descendent par cette matinée
    brûlante de fin d'été
Tous deux sont vêtus de complets couleur kaki et coiffés
    de casques de liège
Tous deux sont suivis d'un domestique noir chargé de
    porter leurs valises
Tous deux jettent le même regard distrait sur les maisons
    trop blanches de la ville sur le ciel trop bleu
On voit le vent soulever des tourbillons de poussière et
    les mouches tourmenter les deux mulets de l'unique
    fiacre
Le cocher dort la bouche ouverte

II. BUNGALOW

L'habitation est petite mais très confortable
La varangue est soutenue par des colonnes de bambou
Des pieds de vanille grimpante s'enroulent tout autour
Des pois d'Angole
Des jasmins
Au-dessus éclatent les magnolias et les corolles des
    flamboyants

La salle à manger est aménagée avec le luxe particulier
    aux créoles de la Caroline
D'énormes blocs de glace dans des vases de marbre
    jaune y maintiennent une fraîcheur délicieuse
La vaisselle plate et les cristaux étincellent
Et derrière chaque convive se tient un serviteur noir

Les invités s'attardent longtemps
Étendus dans des rocking-chairs ils s'abandonnent à ce

SOUTH

I. TAMPA

The train has just come to a stop
Only two travelers get off on this scorching
    late summer morning
Both wear khaki suits and cork helmets
Both are followed by a black servant
    who carries their luggage
Both glance in the same casual way at the houses
    that are too white at the sky that is too blue
You can see the wind raise whirls of dust and the flies
    buzzing around the two mules of the only cab
The cabman is asleep mouth wide open

II. BUNGALOW

The plantation house is small but very comfortable
The floor timbers are supported by bamboo poles
    with creeping vanilla plants twisting all around
Angola peas
Jasmine
Above the magnolias and the poincianas are bursting
    into bloom

Carolina Creole luxury characterizes
    the dining room
Huge blocks of ice in yellow marble vases keep it
    delightfully cool
The silver plate and crystal sparkle
And behind each guest stands a black servant

The guests linger a long time
Lying back in rocking chairs they give in to the

climat amollissant
Sur un signe de son maître le vieux Jupiter sort d'un
    petit meuble laqué
Une bouteille de Xérès
Un seau à glace
Des citrons
Et une boîte de cigares de Pernambuco

Personne ne parlait plus
La sueur ruisselait sur tous les visages
Il n'y avait plus un souffle dans l'air
On entendait dans le lointain le rire énorme de la
    grenouille-taureau qui abonde dans ces parages

III. VOMITO NEGRO

Le paysage n'est plus égayé par des jardins ou des
    forêts
C'est la plaine nue et morne où s'élève à peine de loin
    en loin
Une touffe de bambous
Un saule rabougri
Un eucalyptus tordu par les vents
Puis c'est le marais
Vous voyez ces fumées jaunâtres
Ce brouillard gris au ras du sol agité d'un tressaille-
    ment perpétuel
Ce sont des millions de moustiques et les exhalaisons
    jaunes de la pourriture
Il y a là des endroits où les noirs eux-mêmes ne sauraient
    vivre

De ce côté le rivage est bordé de grands palétuviers
Leurs racines enchevêtrées qui plongent dans la vase
    sont recouvertes de grappes d'huîtres empoisonnées
Les moustiques et les insectes venimeux forment un
    nuage épais au-dessus des eaux croupissantes
A côté des inoffensives grenouilles-taureaux on aperçoit
    des crapauds d'une prodigieuse grosseur

    debilitating climate
At a sign from his master old Jupiter takes out of
    a small lacquered cabinet
A bottle of sherry
An ice bucket
Lemons
And a box of Pernambuco cigars

There was no more talk
Perspiration was streaming down every face
There was no longer a breath of air
In the distance was heard the huge laughter of the
    bullfrog that abounds in these areas

III. VOMITO NEGRO

The landscape is no longer alive with gardens
    or forests
It is the naked and dull plain where
    sparse and scattered hardly grows
A cluster of bamboos
A stunted willow
A blue gum twisted by the winds
Then come the marshes
You see that yellowish haze
That gray fog close to the ground stirring in an
    incessant quiver
It is millions of mosquitoes and the yellow fumes of
    putrefaction
There are places where the blacks themselves
    could not live

On this side of the river tall mangroves grow along the bank
Their entangled roots deeply sunk in mud are covered
    with bunches of poisoned oysters
Mosquitoes and poisonous insects gather in a thick cloud
    over the stagnating waters
Next to the harmless bullfrogs you see fabulously
    large toads

Et ce fameux serpent-cercueil qui donne la chasse à
    ses victimes en gambadant comme un chien
Il y a des mares où pullulent les sangsues couleur ardoise
Les hideux crabes écarlates s'ébattent autour des caïmans
    endormis
Dans les passages où le sol est le plus ferme on rencontre
    des fourmis géantes
Innombrables et voraces

Sur ces eaux pourries dans ces fanges vénéneuses
S'épanouissent des fleurs d'un parfum étourdissant et
    d'une senteur capiteuse et têtue
Éclatent des floraisons d'azur de pourpre
Des feuillages chromés
Partout
L'eau noire se couvre d'un tapis de fleurs que troue la
    tête plate des serpents

J'ai traversé un buisson de grands mimosas
Ils s'écartaient de moi sur mon passage
Ils écartaient leurs branches avec un petit sifflement
Car ce sont des arbres de sensibilité et presque de ner-
    vosité
Au milieu des lianes de jalap pleines de corolles par-
    lantes
Les grands échassiers gris et roses se régalent de lézards
    croustillants et s'envolent avec un grand bruit d'ailes
    à notre approche
Puis ce sont d'immenses papillons aux couleurs de soufre
    de gentiane d'huile lourde
Et des chenilles de taille

IV. RUINE ESPAGNOLE

La nef est construite dans le style espagnol du XVIIIe siècle
Elle est lézardée en de nombreux endroits
La voûte humide est blanche de salpêtre et porte encore
    des traces de dorures

And the famous coffin snake that leaps after its victims
    like a dog
There are ponds teeming with slate-colored leeches
The hideous scarlet crabs play around the sleeping
    alligators
On paths where the ground is most solid
    you find gigantic ants
Innumerable and voracious

Over these putrid waters in that venomous mire
Flowers blossom out with dizzying fragrance
    and a persistent heady scent
Azure and purple break into bloom
Chromed foliage
Everywhere
A flower carpet pockmarked with the snakes' flat heads
    spreads over the black water

I walked through tall mimosa shrubs
They drew aside as I came along
They drew their branches back with a slight hiss
For these are trees with sensitivity with a case
    of nerves almost
In the middle jalap lianas full of talking corollas
The tall gray and pink waders feast on crunchy lizards
    and fly away with a loud flap of wings as we
    come closer
Then come huge butterflies the color of sulfur of
    gentian or heavy oil
And jumbo caterpillars

IV. SPANISH RUIN

The nave is built in the XVIIIth century Spanish style
It is full of cracks
The damp vault is white with saltpeter
    and gilt still shows in places

Les rayons de la lanterne montrent dans un coin un
    tableau moisi
C'est une Vierge Noire
De longues mousses et des champignons vénéneusement
    zébrés pointillés perlés couvrent le pavé du sanctuaire
Il y a aussi une cloche avec des inscriptions latines

V. GOLDEN-GATE

C'est le vieux grillage qui a donné son nom à la maison
Barres de fer grosses comme le poignet qui séparent
    la salle des buveurs du comptoir où sont alignés les
    liqueurs et les alcools de toutes provenances
Au temps où sévissait la fièvre de l'or
Où les femmes amenées par les traitants du Chili ou du
    Mexique se vendaient couramment aux enchères
Tous les bars étaient pourvus de grillages semblables
Alors les barmen ne servaient leurs clients que le revolver
    au poing
Il n'était pas rare qu'un homme fût assassiné pour un
    gobelet
Il est vrai qu'aujourd'hui le grillage n'est plus là que
    pour le pittoresque
Tout de même des Chinois sont là et boivent
Des Allemands des Mexicains
Et aussi quelques Canaques venus avec les petits vapeurs
    chargés de nacre de copra d'écaille de tortues
Chanteuses
Maquillage atroce employés de banque bandits matelots
    aux mains énormes

VI. OYSTER-BAY

Tente de coutil et sièges de bambou
De loin en loin sur ces plages désertes on aperçoit une
    hutte couverte de feuilles de palmier ou l'embarcation
    d'un nègre pêcheur de perles

The rays from the lantern cast light upon a mildewed
    painting in a corner
It is a Black Virgin
Long mosses and venomously veined dotted pearly toadstools
    cover the sanctuary's slabstones
There is also a bell with Latin inscriptions

V. GOLDEN-GATE

It is from the old grille that the place took its name
Iron bars as thick as a wrist screening the public room
    from the bar where bottles of liquor and spirits
    from all places stand in a row
In the days when the gold fever was raging
When women brought by traders from Chile
    or Mexico were usually sold at auction
All the bars were equipped with such grilles
Then barmen would only serve their customers
    gun in hand
It was not rare that a man was shot for a drink
Sure enough the grille is only
    local color now
All the same some Chinese are there drinking
Germans Mexicans
And also a few Melanesians who have come in small
    steamboats laden with mother-of-pearl copra
    tortoiseshell
Girl singers
Atrocious makeup bank clerks gangsters sailors
    with enormous hands

VI. OYSTER-BAY

Canvas tent and bamboo seats
Now and then on those deserted beaches you see a
    hut thatched with palm leaf or the craft of
    a black pearl diver

Maintenant le paysage a changé du tout au tout
A perte de vue
Les plages sont recouvertes d'un sable brillant
Deux ou trois requins s'ébattent dans le sillage du yacht
La Floride disparaît à l'horizon

On prend dans le meuble d'ébène un régalia couleur d'or
On le fait craquer d'un coup d'ongle
On l'allume voluptueusement
Fumez fumeur fumez fumée fait l'hélice

LE NORD

I. PRINTEMPS

Le printemps canadien a une vigueur et une puissance
    que l'on ne trouve dans aucun autre pays du monde
Sous la couche épaisse des neiges et des glaces
Soudainement
La généreuse nature
Touffes de violettes blanches bleues et roses
Orchidées tournesols lis tigrés
Dans les vénérables avenues d'érables de frênes noirs
    et de bouleaux
Les oiseaux volent et chantent
Dans les taillis recouverts de bourgeons et de pousses
    neuves et tendres
Le gai soleil est couleur réglisse

En bordure de la route s'étendent sur une longueur
    de plus de cinq milles les bois et les cultures
C'est un des plus vastes domaines du district de Winnipeg
Au milieu s'élève une ferme solidement construite en
    pierres de taille et qui a des allures de gentilhommière
C'est là que vit mon bon ami Coulon

Now the landscape has radically changed
As far as the eye can see
The beaches are covered with shimmering sand
Two or three sharks gambol in the wake of the yacht
Florida disappears on the horizon

A golden "regalia" is taken from the ebony cabinet
A flick of the nail snaps it
It is lit voluptuously
Smoke smokers smoking smoke whirs the propeller

NORTH

I. SPRING

There is vigor and strength in the Canadian spring
    as in no other country in the world
Under the thick layer of snow and ice
Suddenly
Bountiful nature
Tufts of violets white blue and pink
Orchids sunflowers tiger lilies
In the venerable avenues lined with maple trees
    black ash trees and birches
Birds fly and sing
In the thickets covered with buds and young
    and tender shoots
The cheerful sun is the color of licorice

Alongside the road woods and cultivated lands
    stretch for more than five thousand miles
It is one of the largest estates in the district
    of Winnipeg
In the middle stands a farmhouse solidly built
    of squared stones and looking like a manor
That is where my good friend Coulon lives

Levé avant le jour il chevauche de ferme en ferme monté
sur une haute jument isabelle
Les pattes de son bonnet de peau de lièvre flottent sur
ses épaules
Œil noir et sourcils broussailleux
Tout guilleret
La pipe sur le menton
La nuit est brumeuse et froide
Un furieux vent d'ouest fait gémir les sapins élastiques
et les mélèzes
Une petite lueur va s'élargissant
Un brasier crépite
L'incendie qui couvait dévore les buissons et les brindilles
Le vent tumultueux apporte des bouquets d'arbres
résineux
Coup sur coup d'immenses torches flambent
L'incendie tourne l'horizon avec une imposante lenteur
Troncs blancs et troncs noirs s'ensanglantent
Dôme de fumée chocolat d'où un million d'étincelles
de flammèches jaillissent en tournoyant très haut et
très bas
Derrière ce rideau de flammes on aperçoit des grandes
ombres qui se tordent et s'abattent
Des coups de cognée retentissent
Un âcre brouillard s'étend sur la forêt incandescente
que l'équipe des bûcherons circonscrit

II. CAMPAGNE

Paysage magnifique
Verdoyantes forêts de sapins de hêtres de châtaigniers
coupées de florissantes cultures de blé d'avoine de
sarrasin de chanvre
Tout respire l'abondance
Le pays d'ailleurs est absolument désert
A peine rencontre-t-on par-ci par-là un paysan conduisant
une charrette de fourrage
Dans le lointain les bouleaux sont comme des colonnes
d'argent

Up before dawn he rides a tall light-bay mare
    from farm to farm
The flaps of his hareskin cap dangle on his shoulders
Black eye and bushy eyebrows
In high spirits
A pipe hugging his chin
The night is misty and cold
A wild western wind moans through the elastic fir trees
    and larches
A small gleam of light widens
A fire crackles
The smoldering conflagration burns up bushes and
    brushwood
The tumultuous wind blows about clusters of resinous trees
Huge torches flare up one after the other
The conflagration spreads around the horizon with an
    imposing slowness
White trunks and black trunks turn blood red
Dome of chocolate smoke from which millions of sparks
    flakes of fire fly off high up and low down
Behind the curtain of flames you can see tall shadows
    writhe and drop down
Felling axes bang in the air
An acrid fog spreads over the blazing forest
    circled by the team of woodsmen

II. COUNTRYSIDE

Magnificent landscape
Verdant forests of fir trees beech trees chestnut trees
    interrupted by flourishing fields of wheat oats
    buckwheat hemp
This is a land of plenty
Besides the area is totally deserted
Only occasionally will you meet a peasant driving
    a haycart
In the distance the birches stand like silver pillars

III. PÊCHE ET CHASSE

Canards sauvages pilets sarcelles oies vanneaux outardes
Coqs de bruyère grives
Lièvres arctiques perdrix de neige ptarmigans
Saumons truites arc-en-ciel anguilles
Gigantesques brochets et écrevisses d'une saveur
    particulièrement exquise

La carabine en bandoulière
Le bowie-knife à la ceinture
Le chasseur et le peau-rouge plient sous le poids du
    gibier
Chapelets de ramiers de perdrix rouges
Paons sauvages
Dindons des prairies
Et même un grand aigle blanc et roux descendu des
    nuages

IV. MOISSON

Une six-cylindres et deux Fords au milieu des champs
De tous les côtés et jusqu'à l'horizon les javelles légère-
    ment inclinées tracent un damier de losanges hésitants
Pas un arbre
Du nord descend le tintamarre de la batteuse et de la
    fourragère automobiles
Et du sud montent les douze trains vides qui viennent
    charger le blé

III. FISHING AND HUNTING

Wild ducks pintails teals geese plovers bustards
Grouse thrushes
Arctic hares ptarmigans*
Salmon rainbow trout eels
Gigantic pike and crayfish with a particularly delicate
    flavor

Rifle slung on the shoulder
A bowie knife hanging from the belt
The sportsman and the Red Indian bend under
    their load of game
Wood pigeons red-legged partridges strung on slings
Wild peacocks
Prairie gobblers
And even a large white and russet eagle that
    swooped down from the clouds

IV. HARVEST

A six-cylinder car and two Fords in the middle of
    the fields
In every direction as far as the horizon the slightly
    slanting swaths crisscross into a wavering
    diamond-shaped checkerboard pattern
Not a tree
From the North comes down the rumble and rattle of the
    automative thrasher and forage wagon
And from the South come twelve empty trains to
    pick up the wheat

ILES

I. VICTUAILLES

Le petit port est très animé ce matin
Des coolies — tagals chinois malais — déchargent active-
    ment une grande jonque à poupe dorée et aux voiles
    en bambou tressé
La cargaison se compose de porcelaines venues de la
    grande île de Nippon
De nids d'hirondelles récoltés dans les cavernes de
    Sumatra
D'holothuries
De confitures de gingembre
De pousses de bambou confites dans du vinaigre
Tous les commerçants sont en émoi
Mr. Noghi prétentieusement vêtu d'un complet à
    carreaux de fabrication américaine parle très couram-
    ment l'anglais
C'est en cette langue que s'engage la discussion entre
    ces messieurs
Japonais Canaques Taïtiens Papous Maoris et Fidjiens

II. PROSPECTUS

Visitez notre île
C'est l'île la plus au sud des possessions japonaises
Notre pays est certainement trop peu connu en Europe
Il mérite d'attirer l'attention
La faune et la flore sont très variées et n'ont guère été
    étudiées jusqu'ici
Enfin vous trouverez partout de pittoresques points de
    vue
Et dans l'intérieur
Des ruines de temples bouddhiques qui sont dans leur
    genre de pures merveilles

ISLANDS

I. FARE

There is a lot of activity in the little harbor this morning
Coolies—Tagalogs Chinese Malays—briskly unload a
   large golden-sterned junk with sails made of woven bamboo
The cargo contains porcelain brought from the large
   Nippon island
Swallow's nests gathered in the Sumatra caves
Sea cucumbers
Ginger preserves
Pickled bamboo shoots
Every shopkeeper is all in a flurry
Mr. Noghi pretentiously dressed up in a checked American-
   made suit speaks very fluent English
That's the language in which these gentlemen start their
   business
Japanese Melanesians Tahitians Papuans Maoris and Fijians

II. PUBLICITY

Visit our island
It is the southernmost Japanese territory
Our country is undoubtedly too little known in Europe
It deserves attention
Animal life and plant life are most varied and
   have been hardly studied so far
All in all you will find picturesque vistas everywhere
And inland
Ruins of Buddhist temples which are sheer wonders
   of their kind

III. LA VIPÈRE A CRÊTE ROUGE

A l'aide de la seringue Pravaz il pratique plusieurs
    injections de sérum du docteur Yersin
Puis il agrandit la blessure du bras en pratiquant au
    scalpel une incision cruciale
Il fait saigner la plaie
Puis la cautérise avec quelques gouttes d'hypochlorite
    de chaux

IV. MAISON JAPONAISE

Tiges de bambou
Légères planches
Papier tendu sur des châssis
Il n'existe aucun moyen de chauffage sérieux

V. PETIT JARDIN

Lis chrysanthèmes
Cycas et bananiers
Cerisiers en fleurs
Palmiers orangers et superbes cocotiers chargés de fruits

VI. ROCAILLES

Dans un bassin rempli de dorades de Chine et de pois-
    sons aux gueules monstrueuses
Quelques-uns portent des petits anneaux d'argent
    passés dans les ouïes

VII. LÉGER ET SUBTIL

L'air est embaumé
Musc ambre et fleur de citronnier
Le seul fait d'exister est un véritable bonheur

III. THE RED-CRESTED VIPER

With the hypodermic syringe he makes several
    injections of Dr. Yersin's serum
Then he enlarges the wound in the arm with a
    cross-shaped incision he makes with a scalpel
He draws blood from the cut
Then sears it with a few drops of hypochlorite of lime

IV. JAPANESE HOUSE

Bamboo stalks
Light boards
Paper hung on frames
No heating system to speak of

V. SMALL GARDEN

Lilies chrysanthemums
Cycads and banana trees
Cherry trees in bloom
Palm trees orange trees and magnificent coconut palms
    loaded with fruit

VI. ROCKS

In a pond full of goldfish and other fish with
    monstrous mouths
Some wear small silver rings hanging through their gills

VII. LIGHT AND SUBTILE

Fragrant air
Musk amber and lemon bloom
The mere fact of being is true happiness

VIII. KEEPSAKE

Le ciel et la mer
Les vagues viennent caresser les racines des cocotiers
    et des grands tamarins au feuillage métallique

IX. ANSE POISSONNEUSE

L'eau est si transparente et si calme
On aperçoit dans les profondeurs les broussailles blanches
    des coraux
Le balancement prismatique des méduses suspendues
Les envols des poissons jaunes roses lilas
Et au pied des algues onduleuses les holothuries azurées
    et les oursins verts et violets

X. HATOUARA

Elle ne connaît pas les modes européennes
Crépus et d'un noir bleuâtre ses cheveux sont relevés
    à la japonaise et retenus par des épingles en corail
Elle est nue sous son kimono de soie
Nue jusqu'aux coudes

Lèvres fortes
Yeux langoureux
Nez droit
Teint couleur de cuivre clair
Seins menus
Hanches opulentes

Il y a en elle une vivacité une franchise des mouvements
    et des gestes
Un jeune regard d'animal charmant

Sa science : la grammaire de la démarche

VIII. KEEPSAKE

Sky and sea
Waves flow in and lap the roots of coconut trees and tall
   tamarind trees with metallic leaves

IX. FISH COVE

The water is so clear and so calm
Deep at the bottom you can see the white bushes
   of coral
The prismatic sway of hanging jellyfish
The yellow pink lilac fish taking flight
And at the foot of the wavy seaweeds the azure
   sea cucumbers and the urchins green and purple

X. HATOUARA

She does not know the European fashions
Her frizzy and bluish black hair is gathered up
   in the Japanese manner and held by coral pins
She is naked under her silk kimono
Naked to the elbows

Strong lips
Languorous eyes
Straight nose
Light copper-colored complexion
Tiny breasts
Buxom hips

There is about her a vivacity a freedom of movement
   and gesture
The young look of a charming animal

Her knowledge: the grammar of the art of walking

Elle nage comme on écrit un roman de 400 pages
Infatigable
Hautaine
Aisée
Belle prose soutenue
Elle capture de tout petits poissons qu'elle met dans le
    creux de sa bouche
Puis elle plonge hardiment
Elle file entre les coraux et les varechs polycolores
Pour reparaître bientôt à la surface
Souriante
Tenant à la main deux grosses dorades au ventre d'argent

Toute fière d'une robe de soie bleue toute neuve de
    ses babouches brodées d'or d'un joli collier de corail
    qu'on vient de lui donner le matin même
Elle m'apporte un panier de crabes épineux et fantasques
    et de ces grosses crevettes des mers tropicales que
    l'on appelle des « caraques » et qui sont longues comme
    la main

XI. AMOLLI

Jardin touffu comme une clairière
Sur le rivage paresse l'éternelle chanson bruissante du
    vent dans les feuillages des filaos
Coiffé d'un léger chapeau de rotin armé d'un grand
    parasol de papier
Je contemple les jeux des mouettes et des cormorans
Ou j'examine une fleur
Ou quelque pierre
A chaque geste j'épouvante les écureuils et les rats
    palmistes

Par la fenêtre ouverte je vois la coque allongée d'un
    steamer de moyen tonnage
Ancré à environ deux kilomètres de la côte et qu'entou-
    rent déjà les jonques les sampans et les barques chargés
    de fruits et de marchandises locales

She swims as others write a 400-page novel
Tireless
Haughty
Well-off
Beautiful sustained prose
She catches tiny fish which she puts in the hollow of
    her mouth
Then she dives fearlessly
She glides swiftly among the corals and the multicolored kelp
Soon to reappear on the surface
Smiling
Two big silver-bellied sea breams in her hand

Very proud of a brand-new blue silk dress her Turkish
    slippers embroidered in gold a lovely coral
    necklace she has just been given that morning
She brings me a basket of thorny and temperamental crabs
    and those large tropical sea prawns which people call
    "caracas" and are as long as the hand

XI. NO VIGOR

Bushy garden like a clearing
On the shore the everlasting rustling song of the wind
    idles through the filao leaves
A light rattan hat on my head and armed with a large paper
    parasol
I contemplate the games of the sea gulls and the cormorants
Or I examine a flower
Or some stone
With every movement I startle the chipmunks and the
    palm squirrels

Through the open window I see the elongated hull of
    a steamer of average tonnage
At anchor about two miles away from the coast and already
    surrounded by junks sampans and flatboats carrying
    fruit and local wares

Enfin le soleil se couche
L'air est d'une pureté cristalline
Les mêmes rossignols s'égosillent
Et les grandes chauves-souris vampires passent silen
    cieusement devant la lune sur leurs ailes de velours

Passe une jeune fille complètement nue
La tête couverte d'un de ces anciens casques qui font
    aujourd'hui la joie des collectionneurs
Elle tient à la main un gros bouquet de fleurs pâles
    et d'une pénétrante odeur qui rappelle à la fois la
    tubéreuse et le narcisse
Elle s'arrête court devant la porte du jardin
Des mouches phosphorescentes sont venues se poser
    sur la corne qui somme son casque et ajoutent encore
    au fantastique de l'apparition

Rumeurs nocturnes
Branches mortes qui se cassent
Soupirs de bêtes en rut
Rampements
Bruissements d'insectes
Oiseaux au nid
Voix chuchotées

Les platanes géants sont gris pâle sous la lune
Du sommet de leur voûte retombent des lianes légères
    qu'une bouche invisible balance dans la brise

Les étoiles fondent comme du sucre

FLEUVE

LE BAHR EL-ZERAF

Il n'y a pas de hautes herbes le long des rives
De grandes étendues de terres basses se perdent au loin
Des îles affleurent la surface de l'eau

At last the sun sets
The air is crystal clear
The same nightingales warble on
And the large vampire bats silently glide past the moon on
    their velvet wings

A girl walks by totally in the nude
Her head covered with one of those antique helmets
    which today are a collector's joy
She holds in her hand a large bunch of pale flowers
    with a pervasive fragrance that calls to mind both
    the polianthes and the narcissus
She stops short in front of the garden gate
Phosphorescent flies have settled on the horn that
    tops her helmet and add even more to the
    fantastic character of the apparition

Nocturnal murmurs
Brittle dead branches
Moans of animal in heat
Creeping movements
Insects buzzing
Birds in their nests
Whispering voices
The gigantic plane trees are pale gray in the moon
From their crowning tops hang light lianas
    swayed in the breeze by an invisible mouth

The stars melt like sugar

RIVER

BAHR EL ZERAF

There is no long grass along the banks
Vast expanses of flatlands vanish in the distance
Islands emerge on the surface of the water

De grands crocos se chauffent au soleil
Des milliers de grands oiseaux couvrent les bancs de
de sable ou de boue

Le pays se modifie
Il y a maintenant une brousse assez claire parsemée
d'arbres rachitiques
Il y a des petits oiseaux ravissants de couleur et des
bandes de pintades
Le soir à plusieurs reprises on entend rugir un lion dont
on aperçoit la silhouette sur la rive ouest
J'ai tué ce matin un grand varan d'un mètre et demi
Toujours le même paysage de plaines inondées
Le pilote arabe a aperçu des éléphants
L'intérêt est grand
Tout le monde monte sur le pont supérieur
Pour chacun de nous c'est la première fois que va se
montrer l'empereur des animaux
Les éléphants sont à trois cents mètres environ on en
voit deux gros un moyen trois ou quatre petits
Pendant le déjeuner on signale dix grosses têtes d'hippos
qui nagent devant nous

Le thermomètre ne varie guère
Vers 14 heures il y a régulièrement de 33 à 38°
Le vêtement est costume kaki bonnes chaussures
guêtres et pas de chemise
On fait honneur à la bonne cuisine du bord et aux bou-
teilles de Turin brun
Le soir on ajoute seulement au costume de table un
veston blanc
Milans et vautours passent en nous frôlant de l'aile

Après le dîner le bateau va se placer au milieu du fleuve
pour éviter autant que possible les moustiques
Les rives se déroulent couvertes de papyrus et d'euphor-
bes géants

Big crocodiles bask in the sun
Thousands of large birds cover the sand shoals or
    mudbanks

The landscape changes
Now there is light underbrush with sparse
    stunted trees
There are delightfully colored little birds and
    coveys of guinea fowl
At night you hear repeatedly the roar of a lion
    appearing in outline on the west bank
This morning I killed a big varanian a yard and
    a half long
Still the same landscape of flooded plains
The Arab pilot has spotted elephants
Great interest
Everyone on the upper deck
For all of us it is the first time the king of animals
    will appear
The elephants are about three hundred yards away
    you can see two big ones a medium one three or four
    small ones
During lunch ten big heads of hippos swimming ahead
    of us are announced

The thermometer varies hardly at all
Around 2 P.M. it is regularly between 90° and 100°
We wear khaki suits good shoes gaiters and no shirts
We appreciate the good food on board and the bottles
    of brown Torino
In the evening we add only a white jacket to our
    lunch suits
Kites and vultures brush past us

After dinner the ship sets its course in the middle
    of the river to keep as far away as possible
    from mosquitoes
The banks glide by covered with papyrus and giant
    spurges

Le voyage est lent en suivant les méandres du fleuve
On voit beaucoup d'antilopes et de gazelles peu sauvages
Puis un vieux buffle mais pas de rhinocéros

CHASSE A L'ÉLÉPHANT

I

Terrain infernal
Haute futaie sur marais avec un enchevêtrement de
    lianes et un sous-étage de palmiers bas d'un énorme
    diamètre de feuillage
Piquants droits
Vers midi et demi nous entendons une bande des grands
    animaux que nous cherchons
On perd l'équilibre à chaque instant
L'approche est lente
A peine ai-je aperçu les éléphants qu'ils prennent la
    fuite

II

La nuit
Il y a des éléphants dans les plantations
Au bruit strident des branches cassées arrachées succède
    le bruit plus sourd des gros bananiers renversés d'une
    poussée lente
Nous allons directement sur eux
En montant sur un petit tertre je vois l'avant de la
    bête la plus rapprochée
La lune perpendiculaire l'éclaire favorablement c'est
    un bel éléphant
La trompe en l'air l'extrémité tournée vers moi

It is a slow trip meandering along the curves of the
river
We see many rather tame antelopes and gazelles
Then an old buffalo but no rhinoceros

ELEPHANT HUNTING

I

Ghastly terrain
A forest of tall trees on a marsh with tangled lianas
and an underbrush of low palm trees with an
enormous spread of leaves
Upright thorns
Toward twelve-thirty we hear a herd of the big animals
we are looking for
You lose your balance every minute
Drawing nearer slowly
I hardly catch a glimpse of the elephants
before they run away

II

At night
There are elephants in the plantations
The shrill snap of broken torn-off branches
alternates with the more muffled thud
of large banana trees slowly pushed to
the ground
We proceed directly toward them
Perched on a small mound I see the front of the
nearest animal
The perpendicular moon casts a favorable light upon him
he is a handsome elephant
His trunk turned up the tip toward me

Il m'a senti il ne faut pas perdre une demi-seconde
Le coup part
A l'instant une nouvelle balle passe dans le canon de la
     Winchester
Puis je fume ma pipe
L'énorme bête semble dormir dans la clairière bleue

III

Nous arrivons sur un terrain d'argile
Après avoir pris leur bain de boue les bêtes ont traversé
     des fourrés particulièrement épais
A quinze mètres on ne distingue encore que des masses
     informes sans qu'il soit possible de se rendre compte
     ni de la taille ni des défenses
J'ai rarement aussi bien entendu les bruits intestinaux
     des éléphants leurs ronflements le bruit des branches
     cassées
Tout cela succédant à de longs silences pendant lesquels
     on a peine à croire leur présence si rapprochée

IV

Du campement nous entendons des éléphants dans la
     forêt
Je garde un homme avec moi pour porter le grand kodak
A douze mètres je distingue mal une grande bête
A côté d'elle il me semble voir un petit
Ils sont dans l'eau marécageuse
Littéralement je les entends se gargariser
Le soleil éclaire en plein la tête et le poitrail de la grande
     femelle maintenant irritée
Quelle photo intéressante a pu prendre l'homme de
     sang-froid qui se tenait à côté de moi

He has sniffed me not a split second to lose
Fire
At once a new bullet is fed into the barrel of the Winchester
Then I smoke a pipe
The huge animal seems asleep in the blue clearing

III

We reach clay soil
After taking a mud bath the animals have gone through
    particularly dense thickets
Fifteen yards away you can still see nothing but shapeless
    bulks without being able to make out their size or see
    the tusks
I have seldom heard so clearly the rumbling stomachs of
    elephants
    their snoring the crack of crushed branches
All this after long silences when you can hardly believe
    they are so near

IV

From the camp we hear elephants in the forest
I keep a man by me to carry the large Kodak
Twelve yards away I can barely make out a large animal
Next to it there seems to be a baby one
They stand in marshy water
I literally hear them gargling
The sunlight falls directly on the head and breast
    of the tall female now annoyed
What an interesting snapshot the coolheaded man who stood
    next to me has been able to take

V

Le terrain est impossible
Praticable seulement en suivant les sentiers tracés par
    les éléphants eux-mêmes
Sentiers encombrés d'obstacles de troncs renversés
De lianes que ces puissants animaux enjambent ou bien
    écartent avec leur trompe
Sans jamais les briser ou les supprimer pour ne plus les
    rencontrer sur leur chemin
En cela ils sont comme les indigènes qui n'enlèvent
    pas non plus les obstacles même dans leurs sentiers
    les plus battus

VI

Nous recoupons la piste d'un grand mâle
La bête nous mène droit vers l'ouest tout au travers de
    la grande plaine
Parcourt cinq cents mètres en forêt
Circule quelque temps dans un espace découvert encore
    inconnu de nous
Puis rentre en forêt
Maintenant la bête est parfaitement immobile un ronfle-
    ment trahit seulement sa présence de temps en temps
A dix mètres j'aperçois vaguement quelque chose
Est-ce bien la bête?
Oui voilà bien une énorme dent très blanche
A ce moment une pluie torrentielle se met à tomber
    et une obscurité noire
Le film est raté

VII

Quelquefois les sentiers d'éléphants serpentent se croisent
Enserrés entre des murailles d'arbustes de ronces
Cette végétation est impénétrable même pour les yeux
Elle atteint de trois à six mètres d'élévation

V

The terrain is impossible
Passable only along the trails made by the elephants
   themselves
Trails obstructed with obstacles fallen trunks
Lianas which these powerful animals stride over
   or push aside with their trunks
Without ever breaking or removing them so as not to find
   them again in the way
In that respect they are like the natives who do not
   clear obstacles even from their most
   frequented paths

VI

We come upon the track of a big male
The animal leads us straight toward the west
   all through the vast plain
Cuts through five hundred yards of forest
Roams about for a while in an open space we had not
   discovered yet
Then returns to the forest
Now the animal is perfectly motionless only occasional
   snores revealing his presence
Ten yards off I vaguely distinguish something
   Is that the animal?
Yes indeed here is an enormous very white tooth
Right then torrential rains start to pour and it
   is pitch dark
The film is ruined

VII

Sometimes the elephant trails wind around crisscross
Walled in between shrubs and brambles
Impenetrable growth you can't even see through
Three to six yards high

Dans les sentiers les lianes descendent jusqu'à un deux
    trois pieds du sol
Puis remontent affectant les formes les plus bizarres
Les arbres sont tous énormes le collet de leurs racines
    aériennes est à quatre ou cinq mètres au-dessus du
    terrain

VIII

Nous entendons un troupeau
Il est dans une clairière
Les herbes et les broussailles y atteignent cinq à six mètres
    de haut
Il s'y trouve aussi des espaces restreints dénudés
Je fais rester mes trois hommes sur place chacun braquant
    son Bell-Howel
Et je m'avance seul avec mon petit kodak sur un terrain
    où je puis marcher sans bruit
Il n'y a rien d'aussi drôle que de voir s'élever s'abaisser
    se relever encore
Se contourner en tous sens
Les trompes des éléphants
Dont la tête et tout le corps immense demeurent cachés

IX

J'approche en demi-cercle
Soulevant son énorme tête ornée de grosses défenses
Brassant l'air de ses larges oreilles
La trompe tournée vers moi
Il prend le vent
Une photo et le coup part
L'éléphant reçoit le choc sans broncher
Je répète à toute vitesse
Piquant de la tête il roule à terre avec un râle formidable
Je lui tire ensuite une balle vers le cœur puis deux coups
    dans la tête
Le râle est toujours puissant enfin la vie l'abandonne
J'ai noté la position du cœur et ses dimensions qui sont
    de 55 centimètres de diamètre sur 40

In the trails lianas hang down to one two three feet
  from the ground
Then twist upward again assuming the strangest shapes
The trees are all enormous the collar of their aerial roots
  standing four or five yards above the ground

VIII

We hear a herd
It is in a clearing
The grass and the brush reach five or six yards high
There are also a few barren patches
I order my three men to stand still each
  with his Bell and Howell in focus
And I move forward alone with my little Kodak
  on terrain where my steps won't be heard
There is no funnier sight than elephants swaying their trunks
  up down and up again
Twisting them in all directions
While their heads and their huge bodies remain unseen

IX

I come closer in a half circle
Raising his enormous head with its decorative tusks
His large ears flapping in the air
His trunk aimed at me
He sniffs the wind
A snapshot and then fire
The elephant weathers the shock without a stir
Quick another shot
Head foremost he rolls over with a colossal death rattle
I aim another bullet toward the heart then fire twice
  into the head
The death rattle is still powerful finally life fails him
I noted the heart's position and its dimensions which are
  22 inches by 16

X

Je n'aperçois le bel animal qu'un instant
Maintenant je l'entends patauger pesamment régulière-
    ment
Il froisse les branches sur son passage
C'est une musique grandiose
Il est contre moi et je ne vois rien absolument rien
Tout à coup son énorme tête se dégage des brousssailles
Plein de face
A six mètres
Me dominant
L'éléphant exécute une marche à reculons avec rapidité
A ce moment la pluie se met à tomber avec un fracas
    qui étouffe le bruit des pas

XI

Dans une grande plaine au nord
A la lisière de la forêt une grande femelle un petit mâle
    et trois jeunes éléphants de taille différente
La hauteur des herbes m'empêche de les photographier
Du haut d'une termitière je les observe longtemps avec
    ma jumelle Zeiss
Les éléphants semblent prendre leur dessert avec une
    délicatesse du toucher amusante
Quand les bêtes nous sentent elles détalent
La brousse s'entrouvre pour leur livrer passage et se
    referme comme un rideau sur leurs grosses masses

MENUS

I

Foie de tortue verte truffé
Langouste à la mexicaine
Faisan de la Floride

X

I catch sight of the beautiful animal for a second only
Now I hear him wallowing heavily regularly
He crushes the branches on his way
Splendid music
He stands close to me and I can't see a thing
All of a sudden his huge head emerges from the brush
Full face
Six yards off
Towering over me
The elephant performs a swift backtrack
Right then the rain starts in a clattering downpour
    that drowns the noise of his steps

XI

In a vast northern plain
On the outskirts of the forest a tall female a small male
    and three baby elephants of different sizes
The grass is too high to get a picture
Perched on a termite hill I watch them for a long time
    with my Zeiss field glass
The elephants seem to be eating dessert with a silly
    daintiness of touch
When the beasts scent us they scurry away
The brush opens up to let them pass and closes again
    like a curtain behind their large bulks

MENUS

I

Truffled green tortoise liver
Mexican-style lobster
Florida pheasant

Iguane sauce caraïbe
Gombos et choux palmistes

II

Saumon du Rio Rouge
Jambon d'ours canadien
Roast-beef des prairies du Minnesota
Anguilles fumées
Tomates de San-Francisco
Pale-ale et vins de Californie

III

Saumon de Winnipeg
Jambon de mouton à l'Écossaise
Pommes Royal-Canada
Vieux vins de France

IV

Kankal-Oysters
Salade de homard cœurs de céleris
Escargots de France vanillés au sucre
Poulet de Kentucky
Desserts café whisky canadian-club

V

Ailerons de requin confits dans la saumure
Jeunes chiens mort-nés préparés au miel
Vin de riz aux violettes
Crème au cocon de ver à soie
Vers de terre salés et alcool de Kawa
Confiture d'algues marines

Iguana in Caribbean sauce
Gumbos and palm cabbage

II

Red River salmon
Canadian bear ham
Roast beef from the Minnesota prairies
Smoked eels
San Francisco tomatoes
Pale ale and California wines

III

Winnipeg salmon
Scottish leg o' lamb
Royal Canadian apples
Old wines from France

IV

Kankal oysters
Lobster salad celery hearts
French snails vanilla flavored with sugar
Kentucky fried chicken
Desserts coffee Canadian Club whiskey

V

Pickled shark fins
Stillborn young dogs cured in honey
Violet rice wine
Silkworm cocoon cream
Salted earthworms and kava liqueur
Seaweed preserves

VI

Conserves de bœuf de Chicago et salaisons allemandes
Langouste
Ananas goyaves nèfles du Japon noix de coco mangues
   pomme-crème
Fruits de l'arbre à pain cuits au four

VII

Soupe à la tortue
Huîtres frites
Patte d'ours truffée
Langouste à la Javanaise

VIII

Ragoût de crabes de rivière au piment
Cochon de lait entouré de bananes frites
Hérisson au ravensara
Fruits

En voyage 1887-1923.

VI

Canned Chicago beef and German cured meats
Lobster
Pineapples guavas loquats coconuts mangoes cream-apple
Baked breadfruit

VII

Tortoise soup
Fried oysters
Truffled bear paws
Javanese lobster

VIII

River crab stew with pimiento
Suckling pig with fried bananas all around
Ravensara hedgehog
Fruit

Traveling   1887–1923

A drawing by the Brazilian artist Tarsila do Amaral for the first edition of *Feuilles de route* (Paris: Au Sans Pareil, 1924). *Opposite page:* Tarsila's conception of Cendrars's "Islands" in *Feuilles de route* (Paris: Au Sans Pareil, 1924). [Courtesy of Dr. Guilherme Augusto do Amaral, representative of the heirs of the artist]

FEUILLES DE ROUTE

OCEAN LETTERS

ce cahier est dédié

à

mes bons amis de São-Paulo

Paulo PRADO

Mario Andrade, Serge Millet,

Tasto de Almeida. Couto de Barros,

Rubens de Moraes, Luiz Aranhas,

Oswaldo de Andrade, Yan

et

aux Amis de Rio-de-Janeiro

Graça ARANHA

Sergio Buarque de Hollanda, Prudente

de Moraes, Guillermo de Almeida, Ronald

de Carvalho, Americo Faco

sans oublier

l'inimitable et cher

Leopold de FREITAS

du Rio-Grande-do-Sul

The autographed dedicatory page of Cendrars's *Feuilles de route* in *Du monde entier au coeur du monde* (Paris: Editions Denoël, 1957).

This book is dedicated
to
my good friends in São Paulo
Paulo PRADO
Mario Andrade, Serge Millet
Jasto de Almeida, Conto de Barros
Rubens de Mosaes, Luiz Aranhas,
Oswaldo de Andrade, Yan
and
to my Rio de Janeiro friends
Graza ARANHA
Sergio Buarque de Hollanda, Prudente
de Moraes, Guilhermo de Almeida, Ronald
de Carvalho, Americo Faco
not forgetting
the dear inimitable
Leopold de FREITAS
at the Rio Grande do Sul

I. LE FORMOSE

Voici des années que je n'ai plus pris le train
J'ai fait des randonnées en auto
En avion
Un voyage en mer et j'en refais un autre un plus long

Ce soir me voici tout à coup dans ce bruit de chemin de
    fer qui m'était si familier autrefois
Et il me semble que je le comprends mieux qu'alors

Wagon-restaurant
On ne distingue rien dehors
Il fait nuit noire
Le quart de lune ne bouge pas quand on le regarde
Mais il est tantôt à gauche, tantôt à droite du train

Le rapide fait du 110 à l'heure
Je ne vois rien
Cette sourde stridence qui me fait bourdonner les tym-
    pans — le gauche en est endolori — c'est le passage
    d'une tranchée maçonnée
Puis c'est la cataracte d'un pont métallique
La harpe martelée des aiguilles la gifle d'une gare le
    double crochet à la mâchoire d'un tunnel furibond
Quand le train ralentit à cause des inondations on entend
    un bruit de water-chute et les pistons échauffés de la
    cent tonnes au milieu des bruits de vaisselle et de frein
Le Havre autobus ascenseur

I. THE FORMOSA

ON THE 7:40 P.M. EXPRESS

It has been years since I took a train
I took trips by car
By air
By sea and I am off on another sea voyage a longer one

Here I am this evening all of a sudden in that rumbling of
    trains which I knew so well in the past
And it seems more familiar to me now

Dining car
You can't see a thing outside
It is pitch-dark
The quarter moon does not move when you look at it
But now it is to the left of the train, now to the right

The express is going 75 miles an hour
I can't see a thing
This dull clang that makes my ears buzz—my left eardrum
    aches—it is as we go through a masonry cutting
Then comes the cataract of a metal bridge
The drumming on the harp of the switches the slap of a
    station the double hook to the jaw of an enraged tunnel
When the train slows down because of floods we hear the
    swish of a water chute and the overheated pistons of the
    hundred-ton engine in the midst of the clatter of
    dishes and squeaking brakes
Le Havre bus elevator

J'ouvre les persiennes de la chambre d'hôtel
Je me penche sur les bassins du port et la grande lueur
    froide d'une nuit étoilée
Une femme chatouillée glousse sur le quai
Une chaîne sans fin tousse geint travaille

Je m'endors la fenêtre ouverte sur ce bruit de basse-cour
Comme à la campagne

RÉVEIL

Je dors toujours les fenêtres ouvertes
J'ai dormi comme un homme seul
Les sirènes à vapeur et à air comprimé ne m'ont pas trop
    réveillé

Ce matin je me penche par la fenêtre
Je vois
Le ciel
La mer
La gare maritime par laquelle j'arrivais de New-York en
    1911
La baraque du pilotage
Et
A gauche
Des fumées des cheminées des grues des lampes à arc à
    contre-jour
Le premier tram grelotte dans l'aube glaciale
Moi j'ai trop chaud
Adieu Paris
Bonjour soleil

TU ES PLUS BELLE QUE LE CIEL ET LA MER

Quand tu aimes il faut partir
Quitte ta femme quitte ton enfant
Quitte ton ami quitte ton amie

I open the shutters of the hotel room
I lean out over the harbor's docks and the majestic cold light
    of a starry night
A woman on the wharf chuckles from a tickle
An endless chain coughs moans labors

I fall asleep the window open on that farmyard cackle
    as in the country

WAKING UP

I always sleep with my windows open
I slept like a man alone
The steam foghorns and compressed air sirens did not wake
    me altogether

This morning I lean out of the window
I see
The sky
The sea
The harbor station where I arrived from New York in
    1911
The pilot's cabin
And
On the left
Coils of smoke chimneys cranes arc lamps against the light
The first trolley shivers in the chilly dawn
As for me I am too hot
Farewell Paris
Hello sun

YOU ARE MORE BEAUTIFUL THAN SKY AND SEA

When in love you must go away
Leave your wife leave your child
Leave your boyfriend leave your girl friend

Quitte ton amante quitte ton amant
Quand tu aimes il faut partir

Le monde est plein de nègres et de négresses
Des femmes des hommes des hommes des femmes
Regarde les beaux magasins
Ce fiacre cet homme cette femme ce fiacre
Et toutes les belles marchandises

Il y a l'air il y a le vent
Les montagnes l'eau le ciel la terre
Les enfants les animaux
Les plantes et le charbon de terre

Apprends à vendre à acheter à revendre
Donne prends donne prends
Quand tu aimes il faut savoir
Chanter courir manger boire
Siffler
Et apprendre à travailler

Quand tu aimes il faut partir
Ne larmoie pas en souriant
Ne te niche pas entre deux seins
Respire marche pars va-t-en

Je prends mon bain et je regarde
Je vois la bouche que je connais
La main la jambe Le l'œil
Je prends mon bain et je regarde

Le monde entier est toujours là
La vie pleine de choses surprenantes
Je sors de la pharmacie
Je descends juste de la bascule
Je pèse mes 80 kilos
Je t'aime

Leave the woman you love leave the man you love
When in love you must go away

The world is full of blacks men and women
Women men men women
Look at the beautiful stores
That horsecab that man that woman that horsecab
And all the fine wares

There is the air there is the wind
The mountains the water the sky the earth
The children the animals
The plants and the coal

Learn to sell to buy to resell
Give take give take
When in love you must know
How to sing run eat drink
Whistle
And learn to work

When in love you must go away
Don't have a tearful smile
Don't nestle against breasts
Take a breath move on leave go away

I am taking my bath and look around
I see the mouth I know
The hand the leg the THE EYE
I am taking my bath and look around

The whole world is still there
Life full of astonishing things
I come out of the drugstore
I am just stepping off the scale
I weigh my regular 165 pounds
I love you

LETTRE

Tu m'as dit si tu m'écris
Ne tape pas tout à la machine
Ajoute une ligne de ta main
Un mot un rien oh pas grand'chose
Oui oui oui oui oui oui oui oui

Ma Remington est belle pourtant
Je l'aime beaucoup et travaille bien
Mon écriture est nette et claire
On voit très bien que c'est moi qui l'ai tapée

Il y a des blancs que je suis seul à savoir faire
Vois donc l'œil qu'a ma page
Pourtant pour te faire plaisir j'ajoute à l'encre
Deux trois mots
Et une grosse tache d'encre
Pour que tu ne puisses pas les lire

CLAIR DE LUNE

On tangue on tangue sur le bateau
La lune la lune fait des cercles dans l'eau
Dans le ciel c'est le mât qui fait des cercles
Et désigne toutes les étoiles du doigt
Une jeune Argentine accoudée au bastingage
Rêve à Paris en contemplant les phares qui dessinent la
    côte de France
Rêve à Paris qu'elle ne connaît qu'à peine et qu'elle
    regrette déjà
Ces feux tournants fixes doubles colorés à éclipses lui
    rappellent ceux qu'elle voyait de sa fenêtre d'hôtel sur
    les Boulevards et lui promettent un prompt retour
Elle rêve de revenir bientôt en France et d'habiter Paris
Le bruit de ma machine à écrire l'empêche de mener son
    rêve jusqu'au bout.
Ma belle machine à écrire qui sonne au bout de chaque
    ligne et qui est aussi rapide qu'un jazz

LETTER

You told me if you write
Don't type everything
Add a line in your own hand
A word anything oh nothing much
Yes yes yes yes yes yes yes yes

My Remington is beautiful though
I like it a lot and I work well
My writing is neat and clear
It is very easy to see I am the one who typed it

There are blank spaces I alone know how to make
See the look of my page
Yet to please you I add in ink
Two three words
And a big inkspot
So that you can't read them

MOONLIGHT

Pitching and rolling pitching and rolling
The moon the moon draws circles in the water
In the sky the mast draws circles
And points to every star
A young girl from Argentina leaning over the rails
Dreams of Paris as she gazes at the lighthouse outlining
    the coast of France
Dreams of Paris which she hardly knows and already regrets
These lights revolving steady double colored flashing ones
    remind her of those she saw from her hotel window on
    the boulevards and hold for her the promise of a speedy
    return
She dreams she will soon be back in France and live in Paris
The noise of my typewriter prevents her from completing
    her dream
My beautiful typewriter which rings at the end of every line
    and is as fast as jazz

Ma belle machine à écrire qui m'empêche de rêver à
   bâbord comme à tribord
Et qui me fait suivre jusqu'au bout une idée
Mon idée

LA PALLICE

La Pallice et l'Ile de Ré sont posées sur l'eau et peintes
Minutieusement
Comme ces stores des petits bistros bretons des environs
   de la gare Montparnasse
Ou ces aquarelles infâmes que vend boulevard de la
   Madeleine un rapin hirsute habillé de velours qui a
   les deux mains nouées depuis sa naissance qui peint
   avec les coudes et qui vous fait le boniment à travers
   son bec-de-lièvre
Les vérités de La Pallice

BILBAO

Nous arrivons bien avant l'aube dans la rade de Bilbao
Une crique de montagnes basses et de collines à contre-
   jour noir velours piqué des lumières de la ville
Ce décor simple et bien composé me rappelle et au
   risque de passer pour un imbécile puisque je suis en
   Espagne je le répète me rappelle un décor de Picasso
Il y a des barquettes montées par deux hommes seule-
   ment et munies d'une toute petite voile triangulaire
   qui prennent déjà le large
Deux marsouins font la roue
Dès que le soleil se lève de derrière les montagnes
Ce décor si simple
Est envahi
Par un déluge de couleurs
Qui vont de l'indigo au pourpre
Et qui transforment Picasso en expressionniste allemand
Les extrêmes se touchent

My beautiful typewriter which prevents me from dreaming
   port or starboard
And makes me follow an idea to the end
My idea

LA PALLICE

La Pallice and the Île de Ré are set on the water and painted
With great care
Like the awnings of the small Breton bars around
   Montparnasse Station
Or these distasteful watercolors sold on the boulevard de la
   Madeleine by a shaggy dauber dressed in velvet with
   both hands twisted by congenital paralysis who paints
   with the elbows and spins his yarn through a harelip
The truths of La Pallice*

BILBAO

We reach the Bilbao roadstead well before dawn
A cove with low mountains and hills in dark profile
   against the light velvet dotted with the city lights
This simple and well-composed setting reminds me and at
   the risk of being considered an idiot since I am in
   Spain I repeat it reminds me of a Picasso scene
Dories manned by two men only and equipped with
   a tiny triangular sail are already standing out to sea
Two porpoises are turning somersaults
As soon as the sun comes up behind the mountains
This setting so simple
Is overwhelmed
With a flood of colors
Ranging from indigo to purple
And turning Picasso into a German expressionist
Both ends meet

LA CORUGNA

Un phare attendri comme une madone géante
De l'extérieur c'est une jolie petite ville espagnole
A terre c'est un tas de fumier
Deux trois gratte-ciel y poussent

VILLA GARCIA

Trois croiseurs rapides un navire hôpital
Le pavillon anglais
Des signaux optiques lumineux
Deux carabinieros dorment sur les fauteuils du pont
Enfin nous partons
Dans les vents sucrés

PORTO LEIXOES

On arrive tard et c'est dimanche
Le port est un fleuve déchaîné
Les pauvres émigrants qui attendent que les autorités
    viennent à bord sont rudement secoués dans de pau-
    vres petites barques qui montent les unes sur les autres
    sans couler
Le port a un œil malade l'autre crevé
Et une grue énorme s'incline comme un canon à longue
    portée

SUR LES CÔTES DU PORTUGAL

Du Havre nous n'avons fait que suivre les côtes comme
    les navigateurs anciens
Au large du Portugal la mer est couverte de barques et
    de chalutiers de pêche
Elle est d'un bleu constant et d'une transparence péla-
    gique
Il fait beau et chaud

LA CORUÑA

A lighthouse compassionate like a giant madonna
From outside it is a lovely little Spanish town
Ashore it is a dunghill
Two three skyscrapers spring up on it

VILLAGARCÍA

Three speed cruisers a hospital ship
The Union Jack
Flashing light signals
Two carabineros asleep on deck chairs
Finally we set sail
In sugared winds

PORTO DE LEIXÕES

We get in late and it is Sunday
The harbor is a river in fury
The poor emigrants waiting for the officials to come on board
   get a rough tossing in poor little dinghies that
   pile up on top of one another without sinking
One eye of the harbor is sick the other blind
And a huge crane bends over like a long-range gun

ALONG THE PORTUGUESE COASTS

Since Le Havre we have only hugged the coast like ancient
   mariners
Off Portugal the sea is covered with dories and trawlers
It is a deep sea clear steady blue
The weather is fair and warm

Le soleil tape en plein
D'innombrables algues vertes microscopiques flottent à
la surface
Elles fabriquent des aliments qui leur permettent de se
multiplier rapidement
Elles sont l'inépuisable provende vers laquelle accourt la
légion des infusoires et des larves marines délicates
Animaux de toutes sortes
Vers étoiles de mer oursins
Crustacés menus
Petit monde grouillant près de la surface des eaux toute
pénétrée de lumière
Gourmands et friands
Arrivent les harengs les sardines les maquereaux
Que poursuivent les germons les thons les bonites
Que poursuivent les marsouins les requins les dauphins
Le temps est clair la pêche est favorable
Quand le temps se voile les pêcheurs sont mécontents et
font entendre leurs lamentations jusqu'à la tribune du
parlement.

EN ROUTE POUR DAKAR

L'air est froid
La mer est d'acier
Le ciel est froid
Mon corps est d'acier
Adieu Europe que je quitte pour la première fois depuis
1914
Rien ne m'intéresse plus à ton bord pas plus que les
émigrants de l'entrepont juifs russes basques espagnols
portugais et saltimbanques allemands qui regrettent
Paris
Je veux tout oublier ne plus parler tes langues et coucher
avec des nègres et des négresses des indiens et des
indiennes des animaux des plantes
Et prendre un bain et vivre dans l'eau
Et prendre un bain et vivre dans le soleil en compagnie
d'un gros bananier

The sun beats straight down
Innumerable microscopic green seaweeds float on the
    surface
They manufacture foods that allow them to reproduce
    quickly
They are the inexhaustible provender to which flocks
    the legion of infusorians and delicate marine larvae
Living creatures of all kinds
Worms starfish sea urchins
Tiny shellfish
Small fry swarming near the surface of the waters infused
    with light
Greedy and tasty
Come the herrings the sardines the mackerels
Pursued by the great tunnies the horse mackerels the bonitos
Pursued in turn by the porpoises the sharks the dolphins
It is clear weather good for fishing
When it turns cloudy the fishermen are displeased and make
    their wails resound as far as the floor of Parliament

BOUND FOR DAKAR

The air is cold
The sea is steel
The sky is cold
My body is steel
Farewell Europe which I leave for the first time since 1914
Nothing on board your continent interests me any longer
    anymore than the steerage emigrants Jews Russians Basques
    Spaniards Portuguese and German acrobats who miss Paris
I want to forget everything no longer speak your languages
    and sleep with black men and women Indian men and women
    animals plants
And have a swim and live in the water
And have a swim and live in the sun in the company of a
    big banana tree

Et aimer le gros bourgeon de cette plante
Me segmenter moi-même
Et devenir dur comme un caillou
Tomber à pic
Couler à fond

35° 57′ LATITUDE NORD
15° 16′ LONGITUDE OUEST

C'est aujourd'hui que c'est arrivé
Je guettais l'événement depuis le début de la traversée
La mer était belle avec une grosse houle de fond qui nous
    faisait rouler
Le ciel était couvert depuis le matin
Il était 4 heures de l'après-midi
J'étais en train de jouer aux dominos
Tout à coup je poussai un cri et courus sur le pont
C'est ça c'est ça
Le bleu d'oultremer
Le bleu perroquet du ciel
Atmosphère chaude
On ne sait pas comment cela s'est passé et comment
    définir la chose
Mais tout monte d'un degré de tonalité
Le soir j'en avais la preuve par quatre
Le ciel était maintenant pur
Le soleil couchant comme une roue
La pleine lune comme une autre roue
Et les étoiles plus grandes plus grandes

Ce point se trouve entre Madère à tribord et Casablanca
    à bâbord
Déjà

EN VUE DE L'ILE DE FUERTEVENTURA

Tout a encore grandi depuis hier
L'eau le ciel la pureté de l'atmosphère
Les îles Canaries ont l'aspect des rives du Lac de Côme

And love the big bud of that plant
Cut myself into segments
And become as hard as a stone
Sink straight to the bottom
Drown

35° 57' NORTH LATITUDE
15° 16' WEST LONGITUDE

It happened today
I had been on the lookout since the beginning of the crossing
The sea was fine with a heavy ground swell that made us
    roll
The sky had been overcast since morning
It was 4 P.M.
I was playing dominoes
Suddenly I screamed and ran up on deck
That's it that's it
The ultramarine blue
The parrot blue of the sky
Warm air
You don't know how it happened or how to define it
But everything is pitched in a higher key
At night I was given mathematical proof
The sky was now clear
The setting sun like a wheel
The full moon like another wheel
And the stars larger larger

This point is situated between Madeira to starboard
    and Casablanca to port
So soon

OFF FUERTEVENTURA

Everything has grown still larger since yesterday
The water the sky the purity of the air
The Canary Islands are like the shores of Lake Como

Des traînées de nuages sont comme des glaciers
Il commence à faire chaud

A BORD DU FORMOSE

Le ciel est noir strié de bandes lépreuses
L'eau est noire
Les étoiles grandissent encore et fondent comme des
    cierges larmoyants
Voici ce qui se passe à bord

Sur le gaillard avant quatre Russes sont installés dans
    un paquet de cordages et jouent aux cartes à la lueur
    d'une lanterne vénitienne

Sur la plage avant les Juifs en minorité comme chez eux
    en Pologne se tassent et cèdent le pas aux Espagnols
    qui jouent de la mandoline chantent et dansent la jota

Sur le château les émigrants portugais font une ronde
    paysanne un homme noir frappe deux longues casta-
    gnettes en os et les couples rompent la ronde évoluent
    se retournent frappent du talon tandis qu'une voix
    criarde de femme monte

Les passagers des premières regardent presque tous et
    envient ces jeux populaires

Au salon une Allemande prétentieuse joue du violon
    avec beaucoup de chichi avec beaucoup de chichi une
    jeune Française prétentieuse l'accompagne au piano

Sur le pont-promenade va et vient un Russe mystérieux
    officier de la garde grand-duc incognito personnage à
    la Dostoïewsky que j'ai baptisé Dobro-Vétcher c'est
    un petit bonhomme triste ce soir il est pris d'une
    certaine agitation nerveuse il a mis des escarpins

Trails of clouds look like glaciers
It is getting hot

ON BOARD THE FORMOSA

The sky is black streaked with leprous strips
The water is black
The stars grow still larger and melt like weeping candles
That's what's happening on board

On the forecastle four Russians have settled within a pile
   of ropes and are playing cards by the light of a
   Chinese lantern

On the open deck forward the Jews in a minority as at
   home in Poland huddle together and give way to the
   Spaniards who play the mandolin sing and dance the
   jota

In the deckhouse the Portuguese emigrants dance a country
   round a dark man taps a pair of long bone castanets
   and couples break the circle perform a few steps
   turn around tap their heels while a woman's shrill
   voice rises

The first-class passengers are almost all watching and envy
   these folk games

In the lounge a pretentious German girl is playing the
   violin with much mincing and simpering with much
   mincing and simpering a pretentious French girl
   accompanies her at the piano

On the promenade deck a mysterious Russian paces up
   and down officer of the guard grand duke incognito
   a Dostoevski character I have nicknamed Dobro Vetcher
   he is a sad little man tonight he is seized with a
   kind of nervous agitation he has put on patent leather

vernis un habit à basques et un énorme melon comme
mon père en portait en 1895

Au fumoir on joue aux dominos un jeune médecin qui
ressemble à Jules Romains et qui se rend dans le
haut Soudan un armurier belge qui descendra à
Pernambuco un Hollandais le front coupé en deux
hémisphères par une cicatrice profonde il est directeur
du Mont-de-Piété de Santiago del Chili et une jeune
théâtreuse de Ménilmontant peuple gavrocharde qui
s'occupe d'un tas de combines dans les autos elle
m'offre même une mine de plomb au Brésil et un
puits de pétrole à Bakou

Sur le château-arrière les émigrants allemands bien
propres et soigneusement peignés chantent avec
leurs femmes et leurs enfants des cantiques durs et
des chansons sentimentales

Sur le pont-arrière on discute très fort et se chamaille
dans toutes les langues de l'est européen

Dans la cambuse les Bordelais font une manille et dans
son poste l'opérateur de T. S. F. s'engueule avec
Santander et Mogador

LETTRE-OCÉAN

La lettre-océan n'est pas un nouveau genre poétique
C'est un message pratique à tarif régressif et bien
meilleur marché qu'un radio
On s'en sert beaucoup à bord pour liquider des affaires
que l'on n'a pas eu le temps de régler avant son
départ et pour donner des dernières instructions
C'est également un messager sentimental qui vient vous
dire bonjour de ma part entre deux escales aussi
éloignées que Leixoës et Dakar alors que me sachant
en mer pour six jours on ne s'attend pas à recevoir
de mes nouvelles
Je m'en servirai encore durant la traversée du sud-
atlantique entre Dakar et Rio-de-Janeiro pour porter

pumps a tailcoat and a huge bowler hat the kind my
father used to wear in 1895

In the smoking room people play dominoes a young doctor who
looks like Jules Romains and is going to upper Sudan
a Belgian gunsmith who will get off in Pernambuco
a Dutchman with a forehead split into two hemispheres
by a deep scar he is the director of the municipal
pawnshop in Santiago de Chile and a young ham
actress from Ménilmontant low class sluttish who schemes
all kinds of car deals even offers me a copper mine
in Brazil and an oil well in Baku

On the quarterdeck German emigrants well scrubbed
and neatly combed sing with their wives and
their children stern hymns and sentimental songs

On the afterdeck there is a lot of loud arguing and
squabbling in all the languages of eastern Europe

In the steward's room the boys from Bordeaux are
playing manille and in the radio room the
operator gives hell to Santander and Mogador

OCEAN LETTER

The ocean letter is not a new poetry genre
It is a convenient message with decreasing rates
and much cheaper than a radiogram
It is used a great deal on board to wind up business
there was no time to settle before leaving and
give final instructions
It is also a sentimental messenger who comes and gives
you my greetings between two ports of call as
distant as Leixões and Dakar when knowing I am
for six days at sea one does not expect news from me
I will use it again during the South Atlantic crossing
between Dakar and Rio de Janeiro to send messages

des messages en arrière car on ne peut s'en servir
   que dans ce sens-là
La lettre-océan n'a pas été inventée pour faire de la
   poésie
Mais quand on voyage quand on commerce quand on est
   à bord quand on envoie des lettres-océan
On fait de la poésie

A LA HAUTEUR DU RIO DE L'OURO

Les cormorans nous suivent
Ils ont un vol beaucoup plus sûr que les mouettes ce
   sont des oiseaux beaucoup plus gros ils ont un plus
   beau plumage blanc bordé de noir brun ou tout noir
   comme les corneilles de mer
Nous croisons six petits voiliers chargés de sel qui font
   le service entre Dakar et les Grandes Canaries

EN VUE DU CAP BLANC

L'atmosphère est chaude sans excès
La lumière du soleil filtre à travers un air humide et
   nuageux
La température uniforme est plutôt élevée
C'est la période que traverse sans doute actuellement la
   planète Vénus
Ce sont les meilleures conditions pour paresser

DAKAR

Enfin nous longeons et tournons autour des Deux
   Mamelles qui émergeaient depuis ce matin et gran-
   dissaient sur l'horizon
Nous les contournons et entrons dans le port de Dakar
Quand on se retourne
On voit une digue rouge un ciel bleu et une plage blanche
   éblouissante

backward for that is the only direction in which it
can be used
The ocean letter has not been invented to write poetry
But when traveling when doing business when on board
when sending ocean letters
One writes poetry

OFF RÍO DEL ORO

The cormorants are following us
They fly much more steadily than sea gulls they are
much larger birds they have more beautiful feathers
white with brownish black edges or all black like
sea crows
We pass six small salt-laden sailing boats that ply
between Dakar and the Grand Canary Islands

WHITE CAPE IN SIGHT

The air is not excessively warm
The sunlight sifts through a damp and cloudy atmosphere
The even temperature is rather high
It is the period probably now crossed by the planet
Venus
These are the best conditions for loafing

DAKAR

Finally we are coasting and turning around the Deux
Mamelles which came into view since this morning
and have been rising on the horizon
We sail around them and enter the Dakar harbor
Looking back
You see a red jetty a blue sky and a dazzling white
beach

GORÉE

Un château fort méditerranéen
Et derrière une petite île plate ruines portugaises et
    bungalows d'un jaune moderne très salon d'automne

Dans cet ancien repaire de négriers n'habitent plus que
    les fonctionnaires coloniaux qui ne trouvent pas à
    se loger à Dakar où sévit également la crise des loyers
J'ai visité d'anciens cachots creusés dans la basaltine
    rouge on voit encore les chaînes et les colliers qui
    maintenaient les noirs
Des airs de gramophone descendaient jusque dans ces
    profondeurs

ŒUFS ARTIFICIELS

En attendant de pouvoir débarquer nous buvons des
    cocktails au fumoir
Un banquier nous raconte l'installation et le fonctionne-
    ment d'une fabrique d'œufs artificiels établie dans la
    banlieue de Bordeaux
On fabrique le blanc d'œuf avec de l'hémoglobine de
    sang de cheval
Le jaune d'œuf est fabriqué avec de la farine de maïs
    très impalpable et des huiles fines
Ce mélange est répandu dans des moules ronds qui
    passent au frigorifique
Ainsi on obtient une boule jaune que l'on trempe dans
    du coliure pour qu'une légère pellicule se forme
    autour
On met autour de ce produit de l'hémoglobine fouettée
    comme de la crème et le tout retourne au frigo où le
    blanc d'œuf artificiel se saisit exposé à une température
    très basse
Nouveau bain de coliure puis on obtient par un procédé
    très simple un précipité calcaire qui forme la coquille
Ceci me rappelle que j'ai vu avant la guerre à Düsseldorf
    des machines à polir culotter et nuancer les grains
    de café

GORÉE

A Mediterranean castle
Behind it a small flat island Portuguese ruins and bungalows
    in a very modern Salon d'Automne yellow*
This former slave traders' retreat is inhabited only
    by colonial civil servants who could not find
    lodgings in Dakar where there is also a housing
    crisis
I have visited former cells dug into the red basalt
    you can still see the chains and the iron collars
    that shackled the blacks
Tunes from record players were heard as far down as
    these depths

ARTIFICIAL EGGS

Waiting to go ashore we are having cocktails in the
    smoking room
A banker tells us about the equipment and the functioning
    of an artificial egg factory in the
    suburbs of Bordeaux
The white of the egg is made from horse-blood
    hemoglobin
The yolk is made with powdery cornmeal and refined oils
That mixture is poured into round molds and refrigerated
Thus you get a yellow ball which is dipped into chemicals
    in order to coat it with a light film
That product is covered with hemoglobin whipped like
    cream and the whole thing is placed back in the
    refrigerator where the artificial white of the
    egg sets at a very low temperature
Another chemical dip then a very simple process
    results in a lime precipitate which makes
    up the shell
This reminds me that before the war I saw machines
    in Düsseldorf which polished seasoned and
    tinted coffee beans

Et donner ainsi à des cafés de mauvaise qualité l'aspect
des grains des cafés d'origine Jamaïque Bourbon
    Bornéo Arabie etc.

LES BOUBOUS

Oh ces négresses que l'on rencontre dans les environs
    du village nègre chez les trafiquants qui aunent la
    percale de traite
Aucune femme au monde ne possède cette distinction
    cette noblesse cette démarche cette allure ce port cette
    élégance cette nonchalance ce raffinement cette pro-
    preté cette hygiène cette santé cet optimisme cette
    inconscience cette jeunesse ce goût
Ni l'aristocrate anglaise le matin à Hydepark
Ni l'Espagnole qui se promène le dimanche soir
Ni la belle Romaine du Pincio
Ni les plus belles paysannes de Hongrie ou d'Arménie
Ni la princesse russe raffinée qui passait autrefois en
    traîneau sur les quais de la Néva
Ni la Chinoise d'un bateau de fleurs
Ni les belles dactylos de New-York
Ni même la plus parisienne des Parisiennes
Fasse Dieu que durant toute ma vie ces quelques formes
    entrevues se baladent dans mon cerveau

Chaque mèche de leurs cheveux est une petite tresse de
    la même longueur ointe peinte lustrée
Sur le sommet de la tête elles portent un petit ornement
    de cuir ou d'ivoire qui est maintenu par des fils de
    soie colorés ou des chaînettes de perles vives
Cette coiffure représente des mois de travail et toute leur
    vie se passe à la faire et à la refaire
Des rangs de piécettes d'or percent le cartilage des
    oreilles
Certaines ont des incisions colorées dans le visage sous
    les yeux et dans le cou et toutes se maquillent avec
    un art prodigieux
Leurs mains sont recouvertes de bagues et de bracelets
    et toutes ont les ongles peints ainsi que la paume de
    la main

And thus gave cheap coffee the look of beans guaranteed
   from Jamaica Bourbon Island Borneo Arabia etc.

THE BUBUS

Ah these black women you meet around the black village
   in the shops where calico is measured for trade
No woman in the world has such distinction such nobility
   such a way of walking such bearing such carriage
   such elegance such casual poise such refinement
   such neatness such cleanliness such health such
   optimism such irresponsibility such youth such
   taste
Not the English aristocrat on a Hyde Park morning
Not the Spanish woman on a Sunday evening stroll
Not the handsome Roman woman on the Pincio
Not the most beautiful country girls in Hungary or Armenia
Not the sophisticated Russian princess who used to ride
   in a sleigh along the banks of the Neva
Not the Chinese girl in a flower boat
Not the pretty New York typists
Not even the most Parisian of Parisians
God will that throughout my life those few figures
   I caught sight of may roam about in my mind

Every lock of their hair is a short plait of equal
   length oiled painted lacquered
On top of their heads they wear a small leather or
   ivory ornament held by colored silk threads or
   light chains of bright beads
This hairdo means months of work and they spend
   all their lives doing and undoing it
Rows of little gold coins hang through their ears
Some have colored incisions on the face under the
   eyes and in the neck and all are made up with
   prodigious art
Their hands and arms are covered with rings and bracelets
   and they all have their nails painted as well
   as the palms of their hands

De lourds bracelets d'argent sonnent à leurs chevilles et
    les doigts de pieds sont bagués
Le talon est peint en bleu
Elles s'habillent de boubous de différentes longueurs
    qu'elles portent les uns par-dessus les autres ils sont
    tous d'impression de couleur et de broderies variées
    elles arrivent à composer un ensemble inouï d'un goût
    très sûr où l'orangé le bleu l'or ou le blanc dominent
Elles portent aussi des ceintures et de lourds grigris
D'autres plusieurs turbans célestes
Leur bien le plus précieux est leur dentition impeccable
    et qu'elles astiquent comme on entretient les cuivres
    d'un yacht de luxe
Leur démarche tient également d'un fin voilier
Mais rien ne peut dire les proportions souples de leur
    corps ou exprimer la nonchalance réfléchie de leur
    allure

BIJOU-CONCERT

Non
Jamais plus
Je ne foutrai les pieds dans un beuglant colonial
Je voudrais être ce pauvre nègre je voudrais être ce
    pauvre nègre qui reste à la porte
Car les belles négresses seraient mes sœurs
Et non pas
Et non pas
Ces sales vaches françaises espagnoles serbes allemandes
    qui meublent les loisirs des fonctionnaires cafardeux
    en mal d'un Paris de garnison et qui ne savent com-
    ment tuer le temps
Je voudrais être ce pauvre nègre et perdre mon temps

Heavy silver bracelets tinkle at their ankles and
    their toes are adorned with rings
The heels are painted blue
They dress in bubus of different lengths which they wear
    on top of one another all are made of colored prints
    and varied embroideries they manage to create an
    astonishing arrangement of perfect taste where
    orange blue gold and white predominate
They also wear belts and heavy amulets
Some wear celestial turbans
Their most precious possession is their perfect
    teeth which they polish like brass on a luxury yacht
Their walk suggests the movement of an elegant clipper
But nothing can convey the supple proportions of their bodies
    or express the measured casual poise of their looks

GEM CONCERT

No
Never again
Will they see my ass in a colonial rowdy joint
I would like to be this poor black man I would
    like to be this poor black man who stays
    at the door
For then the beautiful black women would be my
    sisters
And surely not
Surely not
These lousy bitches French Spanish Serbian German
    who fill up the leisure time of the dumpish
    civil servants homesick for garrison time in
    Paris and who do not know how to kill time
I would like to be that poor black man and waste
    my time

LES CHAROGNARDS

Le village nègre est moins moche est moins sale que la
zone de Saint-Ouen
Les charognards qui le survolent plongent parfois et le
nettoient

SOUS LES TROPIQUES

Dans ces parages le courant des vagues couvre les
rochers d'une abondante floraison animale
Des éponges de toutes sortes
Des polypes si semblables par leur forme à des plantes
qu'on les appelle
Des « lys de mer » quand ils ont l'air de fleurs vivantes
fixées au fond de la mer par leur pédoncule
Des « palmiers marins » quand ils étalent au sommet
d'une tige qui peut atteindre 17 mètres leur panache
de bras semblables à des feuilles de dattiers
Les uns ont cinq bras d'autres en ont dix semblables à
des plumes couleur de rose et nagent en les faisant
onduler
Sur les récifs d'innombrables mollusques traînent leur
coquille dont la variété est infinie
Aux formes surbaissées et à bouche arrondie sont venues
s'ajouter les longues coquilles aux tours d'hélice nom-
breux
La coquille renflée et polie
Celle à longue ouverture évasée échancrée ou prolongée
en canal
Et le mollusque qui vole dans l'eau à l'aide de deux larges
ailes dépendantes de son pied qui vole dans la haute
mer comme les papillons volent dans l'air

ORNITHICHNITES

Les oiseaux qui nous suivaient continuellement depuis
Le Havre disparaissent aujourd'hui

THE VULTURES

The black village is less shabby is less dirty
   than the Saint-Ouen slum area
The vultures that hover over it swoop down from
   time to time and clean it up

IN THE TROPICS

In these regions the tidal waves cover the rocks
   with an abundant animal growth
Sponges of all kinds
Polyps shaped so much like plants that they are called
"Sea lilies" when they look like living flowers attached
   to the bottom of the sea by their stalks
"Marine palms" when at the top of a stem which may be
   17 yards long they spread a tuft of arms like
   palm leaves
Some have five arms others ten similar to rose-colored
   feathers and wave them as they swim
On the reefs innumerable mollusks drag their shells of
   infinite variety
The flattened shapes with rounded mouths have been
   joined by the long shells with numerous spiral
   turns
The glossy ventricose shell
The one with a long opening funnel-shaped scalloped
   or extending into a canal
And the mollusk which flies in water with two wide
   wings activated by its foot which flies in the
   high seas as butterflies in the air

ORNITHICHNITES

The birds that have followed us all the time since Le Havre
   disappear today

Par contre à l'avant s'envolent des bandes de poissons-
   volants que le vent projette sur le pont
Ce sont de tout petits êtres qui sentent terriblement
   mauvais
Leur membrane est gluante

BLEUS

La mer est comme un ciel bleu bleu bleu
Par au-dessus le ciel est comme le Lac Léman
Bleu-tendre

COUCHERS DE SOLEIL

Tout le monde parle des couchers de soleil
Tous les voyageurs sont d'accord pour parler des cou-
   chers de soleil dans ces parages
Il y a plein de bouquins où l'on ne décrit que les couchers
   de soleil
Les couchers de soleil des tropiques
Oui c'est vrai c'est splendide
Mais je préfère de beaucoup les levers de soleil
L'aube
Je n'en rate pas une
Je suis toujours sur le pont
A poils
Et je suis toujours seul à les admirer
Mais je ne vais pas les décrire les aubes
Je vais les garder pour moi seul

NUITS ÉTOILÉES

Je passe la plus grande partie de la nuit sur le pont
Les étoiles familières de nos latitudes penchent penchent
   sur le ciel
L'étoile Polaire descend de plus en plus sur l'horizon nord

On the other hand at the bow schools of flying fish
   fly off and are blown on deck by the wind
They are tiny creatures with a terrible stench
Their membrane is gluey

BLUES

The sea is like a sky blue blue blue
Overhead the sky is like Lake Leman
Soft blue

SUNSETS

Everybody talks about sunsets
All the passengers agree to talk about sunsets
   in these areas
There are loads of books describing nothing but
   sunsets
Sunsets in the tropics
Yes that's right it is magnificent
But I much prefer the sunrises
Dawn
I never miss one
I am always on deck
Without a stitch on
And I am always alone to admire them
But I am not about to describe the dawns
I am going to keep them for myself alone

STARRY NIGHTS

I spend the greater part of the night on deck
The familiar stars of our latitudes lean lean
   over the sky
The polestar comes farther and farther down
   on the northern horizon

Orion — ma constellation — est au zénith
La Voie Lactée comme une fente lumineuse s'élargit
    chaque nuit
Le Chariot est une petite brume
Le sud est de plus en plus noir devant nous
Et j'attends avec impatience l'apparition de la Croix du
    Sud à l'est
Pour me faire patienter Vénus a doublé de grandeur et
    quintuplé d'éclat comme la lune elle fait une traînée
    sur la mer
Cette nuit j'ai vu tomber un bolide

COMPLET BLANC

Je me promène sur le pont dans mon complet blanc
    acheté à Dakar
Aux pieds j'ai mes espadrilles achetées à Villa Garcia
Je tiens à la main mon bonnet basque rapporté de
    Biarritz
Mes poches sont pleines de Caporal Ordinaire
De temps en temps je flaire mon étui en bois de Russie
Je fais sonner des sous dans ma poche et une livre sterling
    en or
J'ai mon gros mouchoir calabrais et des allumettes de
    cire de ces grosses que l'on ne trouve qu'à Londres
Je suis propre lavé frotté plus que le pont
Heureux comme un roi
Riche comme un milliardaire
Libre comme un homme

LA CABINE Nº 6

Je l'occupe
Je devrais toujours vivre ici
Je n'ai aucun mérite à y rester enfermé et à travailler
D'ailleurs je ne travaille pas j'écris tout ce qui me passe
    par la tête

Orion—my constellation—has reached its zenith
The Milky Way like a luminous slit widens every night
The Great Bear is a small mist
The south becomes darker and darker ahead of us
And I am anxiously waiting for the Southern Cross
    to appear in the east
To help me wait patiently Venus has become twice as
    large and five times brighter like the moon it
    sheds a trail of light on the sea
Tonight I saw a meteor fall

WHITE SUIT

I am walking on deck in the white suit I bought
    in Dakar
On my feet I have the canvas and rope shoes I
    bought in Villagarcía
I hold in my hand the Basque beret I brought back
    from Biarritz
My pockets are filled with regular Caporal cigarettes
Now and then I sniff my Russian wood cigarette case
I jingle the coins in my pocket and a gold pound
    sterling
I have my large handkerchief from Calabria and wax
    matches those big ones you find only in London
I am clean washed and scrubbed more than the deck
Happy as a king
Rich as a multimillionaire
Free as a man

CABIN 6

It's mine
I should always live here
I deserve no praise for staying locked up working
    in here
Besides I am not working I write all that comes to
    my mind

Non tout de même pas tout
Car des tas de choses me passent par la tête mais n'entrent
   pas dans ma cabine
Je vis dans un courant d'air le hublot grand ouvert et
   le ventilateur ronflant
Je ne lis rien

BAGAGE

Dire que des gens voyagent avec des tas de bagages
Moi je n'ai emporté que ma malle de cabine et déjà je
   trouve que c'est trop que j'ai trop de choses
Voici ce que ma malle contient
Le manuscrit de Moravagine que je dois terminer à bord
   et mettre à la poste à Santos pour l'expédier à Grasset
Le manuscrit du Plan de l'Aiguille que je dois terminer
   le plus tôt possible pour l'expédier au Sans Pareil
Le manuscrit d'un ballet pour la prochaine saison des
   Ballets Suédois et que j'ai fait à bord entre Le Havre
   et La Pallice d'où je l'ai envoyé à Satie
Le manuscrit du Cœur du Monde que j'enverrai au fur
   et à mesure à Raymone
Le manuscrit de l'Équatoria
Un gros paquet de contes nègres qui formera le deuxième
   volume de mon Anthologie
Plusieurs dossiers d'affaires
Les deux gros volumes du dictionnaire Darmesteter
Ma Remington portable dernier modèle
Un paquet contenant des petites choses que je dois
   remettre à une femme à Rio
Mes babouches de Tombouctou qui portent les marques
   de la grande caravane
Deux paires de godasses mirifiques
Une paire de vernis
Deux complets
Deux pardessus

No not everything all the same
For lots of things come to my mind but do not enter
    my cabin
I live in a draft the porthole wide open and the fan
    whirring
I don't read a thing

LUGGAGE

To think that some people travel with loads of luggage
As for me I have taken only my steamer trunk and already
    I feel it is too much that I have too much junk
Here are the contents of my trunk
The manuscript of Moravagine which I must complete on
    board and mail in Santos to send it to Grasset
The manuscript of the Plan de l'aiguille which I must
    complete as soon as possible and send to
    Sans Pareil
The manuscript of a ballet for the next season of the
    Swedish Ballet Company which I wrote on board
    between Le Havre and La Pallice where I mailed it
    to Satie
The manuscript of Coeur du Monde which I'll gradually
    send to Raymone
The manuscript of Equatoria*
A big package of African tales which will constitute
    the second volume of my Anthology
Several business files
The two large volumes of the Darmesteter dictionary
My portable Remington latest model
A package with some odds and ends I must deliver to
    some woman in Rio
My Turkish slippers from Tumbuctoo that bear the imprint
    of the Great Caravan
Two pairs of smashing brogues
One pair of patent leather shoes
Two suits
Two overcoats

Mon gros chandail du Mont-Blanc
De menus objets pour la toilette
Une cravate
Six douzaines de mouchoirs
Trois liquettes
Six pyjamas
Des kilos de papier blanc
Des kilos de papier blanc
Et un grigri
Ma malle pèse 57 kilos sans mon galurin gris

ORION

C'est mon étoile
Elle a la forme d'une main
C'est ma main montée au ciel
Durant toute la guerre je voyais Orion par un créneau
Quand les Zeppelins venaient bombarder Paris ils
    venaient toujours d'Orion
Aujourd'hui je l'ai au-dessus de ma tête
Le grand mât perce la paume de cette main qui doit
    souffrir
Comme ma main coupée me fait souffrir percée qu'elle
    est par un dard continuel

L'ÉQUATEUR

L'océan est d'un bleu noir le ciel bleu est pâle à côté
La mer se renfle tout autour de l'horizon
On dirait que l'Atlantique va déborder sur le ciel
Tout autour du paquebot c'est une cuve d'outremer pur

My big Mont Blanc sweater
A few toilet articles
A tie
Six dozen handkerchiefs
Three shirts
Six pairs of pajamas
Pounds of white paper
Pounds of white paper
And an amulet
My trunk weighs 115 pounds without my gray hat

ORION

That is my star
It is shaped like a hand
That is my hand gone up to heaven
During the entire war I saw Orion through a lookout
    slit
When the Zeppelins came to bombard Paris they always
    came from Orion
Today it is above my head
The mainmast goes through the palm of that hand
    which must feel pain
Just as my amputated hand hurts pierced as it is
    by a continuous sting

EQUATOR

The ocean is blue-black the blue sky is pale next
    to it
The sea swells out all around the horizon
It looks as if the Atlantic were to overflow on the sky
All around the liner is a vat of pure ultramarine

LE PASSAGE DE LA LIGNE

Naturellement j'ai été baptisé
C'est mon onzième baptême de la ligne
Je m'étais habillé en femme et l'on a bien rigolé
Puis on a bu

JE NAGE

Jusqu'à la ligne c'était l'hiver
Maintenant c'est l'été
Le commandant a fait installer une piscine sur le pont
    supérieur
Je plonge je nage je fais la planche
Je n'écris plus
Il fait bon vivre

S. FERNANDO DE NORONHA

J'envoie un radio à Santos pour annoncer mon arrivée
Puis je remonte me mettre dans la piscine
Comme j'étais en train de nager sur le dos et de faire la
    baleine M. Mouton l'officier radiotélégraphiste du bord
    m'annonce qu'il est en communication avec le « Belle-
    Isle » et me demande si je ne veux pas envoyer une
    lettre-océan (à Mme Raymone ajoute-t-il avec un
    beau sourire)
J'envoie une lettre-océan pour dire qu'il fait bon vivre
Et je me remets dans l'eau
L'eau est fraîche
L'eau est salée

AMARALINA

Ce poste de T. S. F. me fait dire qu'on m'attendra à
    Santos avec une auto
Je suis désespéré d'être bientôt arrivé

CROSSING THE LINE

Naturally I have been ducked
It is my eleventh crossing of the line
I was dressed as a woman and we had a lot of fun
Then we drank

I SWIM

Down to the line it was winter
Now it is summer
The captain had a swimming pool set up on the
    upper deck
I dive I swim I float on my back
I don't write anymore
Life is good to live

S. FERNANDO DE NORONHA

I send a telegram to Santos to announce my arrival
Then I go back up into the pool
As I was swimming on my back and playing the whale
    M. Mouton the radio officer on board informs
    me he has got the "Belle-Isle" and asks me
    whether I wish to send an ocean letter (to Madame
    Raymone he adds with a beautiful smile)
I send an ocean letter to say life is good to live
And I get back into the water
The water is cool
The water is salty

AMARALINA

A radiogram informs me I will be met in Santos
    with a car
I can't bear the idea of arriving so soon

Encore six jours de mer seulement
J'ai le cafard
Je ne voudrais jamais arriver et faire sauter la Western

LES SOUFFLEURS

Nous sommes à la hauteur de Bahia
J'ai vu un premier oiseau
Un cargo anglais
Et trois souffleurs au large
J'ai aussi vu une grande dorade

DIMANCHE

Il fait dimanche sur l'eau
Il fait chaud
Je suis dans ma cabine enfermé comme dans du beurre
   fondant

LE POTEAU NOIR

Nous sommes depuis plusieurs jours déjà dans la région
   du poteau
Je sais bien que l'on écrit depuis toujours le pot au noir
Mais ici à bord on dit le poteau
Le poteau est un poteau noir au milieu de l'océan où
   tous les bateaux s'arrêtent histoire de mettre une
   lettre à la poste
Le poteau est un poteau noir enduit de goudron où l'on
   attachait autrefois les matelots punis de corde ou de
   schlague
Le poteau est un poteau noir contre lequel vient se frotter
   le chat à neuf queues
Assurément quand l'orage est sur vous on est comme dans
   un pot de noir
Mais quand l'orage se forme on voit une barre noire
   dans le ciel cette barre noircit s'avance menace et
   dame le matelot le matelot qui n'a pas la conscience
   tranquille pense au poteau noir

Only six more days at sea
I'm blue
I wish never to arrive I'd like to blow up Western Union

BLOWERS

We are off Bahia
I saw the first bird
An English cargo boat
And three blowers in the offing
I saw a big dolphin too

SUNDAY

It is Sunday on the water
It's hot
I am in my cabin locked up as in melting butter

THE PITCH POLE*

We have already been for several days in the pitch-pole area
I know that it has always been called the pitch pot
But here on board we say the pitch pole
The pole is a black pole in the middle of the ocean
    where all the ships stop just to mail a letter
The pole is a black tarred pole where sailors used
    to be tied up when punished with rope or flogging
The pole is a black pole against which the cat-o'-nine-tails
    comes to rub
Sure enough when the thunderstorm is over it is like being
    in a pot of pitch black
But when the storm is brewing you see a pitch-black bar
    in the sky that bar darkens moves forward threatens
    and golly the sailor the sailor with a guilty conscience
    thinks of the pitch-black pole

D'ailleurs même si j'ai tort j'écrirai le poteau noir et
   non le pot au noir car j'aime le parler populaire et
   rien ne me prouve que ce terme n'est pas en train
   de muer
Et tous les hommes du Formose me donnent raison

PEDRO ALVAREZ CABRAL

Le Portugais Pedro Alvarez Cabral s'était embarqué à
   Lisbonne
En l'année 1500
Pour se rendre dans les Indes Orientales
Des vents contraires le portèrent vers l'ouest et le Brésil
   fut découvert

TERRES

Un cargo pointe vers Pernambuco
Dans la lorgnette du barman c'est un vapeur anglais
   tout recouvert de toiles blanches
A l'œil nu il paraît enfoncé dans l'eau et cassé par le
   milieu comme la série des cargos américains construits
   durant la guerre
On discute ferme à ce sujet quand j'aperçois la côte
C'est une terre arrondie entourée de vapeurs chromées et
   surmontée de trois panaches de nacre
Deux heures plus tard nous voyons des montagnes
   triangulaires
Bleues et noires

ŒUFS

La côte du Brésil est semée d'îlots ronds nus au milieu
   desquels nous naviguons depuis deux jours
On dirait des œufs bigarrés qu'un gigantesque oiseau a
   laissés choir
Ou des fientes volcaniques
Ou des sphingtéas de vautour

At any rate even if I am wrong I'll write the pitch pole and
    not the pitch pot because I like the common language and
    nothing proves to me that the term is not undergoing
    some change
And all the men aboard the *Formosa* agree with me

PEDRO ALVARES CABRAL

The Portuguese sailor Pedro Alvares Cabral embarked in
    Lisbon
In the year 1500
Bound for the East Indies
Contrary winds took him westward and Brazil was
    discovered

LANDS

A freighter heads for Pernambuco
In the barman's binoculars it is an English steamer
    all covered with white canvas
To the naked eye she looks deeply sunk in water and
    indented in the middle like numbers of American
    freighters built during the war
We are busy arguing about this matter when I see the coast
It is a rounded land surrounded by chromed mists and topped
    with three mother-of-pearl plumes
Two hours later we see triangular mountains
Blue and black

EGGS

The coast of Brazil is strewn with round barren islets
    among which we have been sailing for two days
They look like mottled eggs dropped by a gigantic bird
Or volcanic dung
Or vultures' droppings

PAPILLON

C'est curieux
Depuis deux jours que nous sommes en vue des terres
    aucun oiseau n'est venu à notre rencontre ou se mettre
    dans notre sillage
Par contre
Aujourd'hui
A l'aube
Comme nous pénétrions dans la baie de Rio
Un papillon grand comme la main est venu virevolter
    tout autour du paquebot
Il était noir et jaune avec de grandes stries d'un bleu
    déteint

RIO DE JANEIRO

Tout le monde est sur le pont
Nous sommes au milieu des montagnes
Un phare s'éteint
On cherche le Pain de Sucre partout et dix personnes le
    découvrent à la fois dans cent directions différentes
    tant ces montagnes se ressemblent dans leur piriformité
M. Lopart me montre une montagne qui se profile sur
    le ciel comme un cadavre étendu et dont la silhouette
    ressemble beaucoup à celle de Napoléon sur son lit
    de mort
Je trouve qu'elle ressemble plutôt à Wagner un Richard
    Wagner bouffi d'orgueil ou envahi par la graisse
Rio est maintenant tout près et l'on distingue les maisons
    sur la plage
Les officiers comparent ce panorama à celui de la Corne
    d'Or
D'autres racontent la révolte des forts
D'autres regrettent unanimement la construction d'un
    grand hôtel moderne haut et carré qui défigure la baie
    (il est très beau)
D'autres encore protestent véhémentement contre l'abra-
    sage d'une montagne

BUTTERFLY

It is strange
For the two days we have been within sight of land
   no bird has come to meet us or follow in our
   wake
On the other hand
Today
At dawn
As we were entering the bay of Rio
A butterfly as big as a hand came flitting about
   the liner
It was black and yellow with large faded blue streaks

RIO DE JANEIRO

Everyone is on deck
We are surrounded by mountains
A beacon goes out
People look for the Sugar Loaf everywhere and ten discover
   it at the same time in a hundred different directions
   so much alike are these pear-shaped mountains
M. Lopart shows me a mountain outlined against the sky
   like a recumbent corpse whose profile looks a lot
   like Napoleon's on his deathbed
I think it rather looks like Wagner a Richard Wagner
   puffed up with pride or overwhelmed with fat
Rio is now very close and you can make out the houses
   on the beach
The officers compare this panorama with that of the
   Golden Horn
Others tell about the rebellion of the forts
Others unanimously regret the construction of a big
   high square modern hotel which mars the bay
   (it is a very beautiful hotel)
Still others vehemently protest the razing of a mountain

Penché sur le bastingage tribord je contemple
La végétation tropicale d'un îlot abandonné
Le grand soleil qui creuse la grande végétation
Une petite barque montée par trois pêcheurs
Ces hommes aux mouvements lents et méthodiques
Qui travaillent
Qui pêchent
Qui attrapent du poisson
Qui ne nous regardent même pas
Tout à leur métier

SUR RADE

On a hissé les pavillons
Le jaune pour demander la visite de la santé
Le bleu pour demander la police
Le rouge et blanc pour demander la douane
Celui constellé des Chargeurs Réunis
Et le bleu blanc rouge
Et le brésilien
Il y en a encore deux que je ne connais pas
Les passagers admirent les constructions déconfites de
    l'Exposition
Des vedettes des ferrys vont viennent et des grandes
    voiles latines très lentes comme sur le lac de Genève
Le soleil tape
Un aigle tombe

LA COUPÉE

On est enfin à quai un quai rectiligne moderne armé de
    grues de Duisburg
Des mouchoirs s'agitent
On se fait des signes
Blanc-boubou-boubou-blanc m'a déjà oublié
Elle découvre dans la foule un long zigoto cuivré très chic
    et indolent que je crois bien avoir déjà rencontré à Paris

Leaning over the starboard railing I contemplate
The tropical growth on a deserted island
The great sun furrowing into the tall vegetation
A little dory with three fishermen
These men with slow methodical movements
Who work
Who fish
Who catch fish
Who don't even look at us
Fully on the job

IN THE ROADSTEADS

The flags have been hoisted
Yellow to request health inspectors
Blue to request the police
Red and white to request customs officers
The starry one of the Chargeurs Réunis
And the blue white and red
And the Brazilian
There are still two more that I don't know
The passengers admire the nonplussed Exposition buildings
Launches ferry boats come and go and large lateen sails
    very slow as on the lake of Geneva
The sun beats down
An eagle falls

THE GANGWAY

We finally docked at a straight modern pier equipped
    with cranes from Duisburg
Handkerchiefs wave
People make signs to one another
Blanc-boubou-boubou-blanc has already forgotten me
She spots in the crowd a tall copper-skinned guy very
    fashionable and indolent whom I am pretty sure
    I have already met in Paris

Elle est émue c'est beau puis lui fait signe de retenir un
    porteur et lui fait comprendre par cris et par gestes
    qu'elle a cinq malles de cabine et beaucoup beaucoup
    d'autres bagages des grands et des petits
Moi je sais même tout ce qu'elle a dans ces malles car je
    les lui ai bouclées ce matin alors qu'elle avait presque
    une crise de nerfs
Au revoir gosselette gosseline elle passe maintenant la
    coupée au bras de son type fin comme un chevreuil
    inquiétant et attirant
Comme tout mélange princier de sang blanc et noir
Je songe au grand grigri créole qu'il porte dans sa culotte
Une voix monte du quai Est-ce que Monsieur Blaise
    Cendrars est à bord?
Présent!
Douze chapeaux s'agitent
Je débarque
Et l'on me photographie
« Monte là-dessus... Monte là-dessus... »

BANQUET

Une heure de taxi le long de la plage
Vitesse klaxon présentations rires jeunes gens Paris
    Rio Brésil France interviews présentations rires
Nous allons jusqu'à la Grotte de la Presse
Puis nous rentrons déjeuner en ville
Les plats ne sont pas encore servis que déjà les journaux
    parlent de moi et publient la photo de tout à l'heure
Bonne cuisine du pays vins portugais et pinga
A quatorze heures tapantes je suis à bord
Un jeune poète sympathique dégobille sur le pont je
    le ramène à terre où son compagnon dégobille à son
    tour
Les autres n'ont pu suivre
Je monte me plonger dans la piscine tandis que le For-
    mose appareille
Vive l'eau

She is excited that's great then she motions to him
   to get a porter shouting and gesticulating she
   makes him understand that she has five steamer
   trunks and many many more pieces of luggage
   large and small
But I even know all she has in those trunks
   because I closed them up for her this morning
   when she was almost losing her mind
Good-bye kiddo-kiddy she is now walking down the gangway
   on the arm of her chap slender like a deer
   disquieting and attractive
Like every princely mixture of black and white blood
I think of the large Creole amulet he wears in his underpants
A voice rises from the pier Is Monsieur Blaise Cendrars
   on board?
Here!
Twelve hats are waved
I disembark
And pictures are taken of me
"Get up here . . . Get up here . . ."

BANQUET

An hour's taxi ride along the beach
Speed horns introductions laughter young men Paris Rio
   Brazil France interviews introductions laughter
We drive as far as the Press Grotto
Then return to the city for lunch
The food has not been served yet and the newspapers
   already speak about me and print the picture
   they just took
Good local food Portuguese wines and pinga
At two P.M. sharp I am on board
An engaging young poet throws up on deck I take him
   back ashore where his friend throws up too
The others could not keep up
I go up for a dip in the pool while the *Formosa*
   gets underway
Nothing like water

BELLE SOIRÉE

Le soir tombe sur la côte américaine
Pas un poisson pas un oiseau
Une chaîne continue de montagnes uniformes toutes
    recouvertes d'une végétation luxuriante
La mer est unie
Le ciel aussi
Je pense aux deux amis que je me suis fait à bord et qui
    viennent de me quitter à Rio
M. Lopart agent de change à Bruxelles gentil charmant
    qui me tenait tête à table ou le soir au fumoir devant
    une bouteille de whisky
Et Boubou-blanc-blanc-boubou la meilleure des copines
    avec qui je nageais des heures dans la piscine matin
    et soir
A nous trois nous faisions un groupe très gai qui pleurait
    aux larmes à force de rire
Nous avons embêté tout le monde à bord scandalisé les
    fonctionnaires et militaires (supérieurs) en mission
Je n'ai jamais autant ri depuis dix ans et ri durant
    vingt jours j'étais malade de rire et ai augmenté de
    six kilos
Au revoir mes bons amis à bientôt nous nous retrouverons
    à bord en rentrant en France ou un autre jour à Paris
    ou à Bruxelles ou ailleurs dans un train qui franchira
    les Andes ou à bord de l'Emperess qui cinglera vers
    l'Australie nous aurons toujours le même barman car
    le monde est bien petit pour d'aussi gais compagnons.
A bientôt à bientôt

PLEINE NUIT EN MER

La côte montagneuse est éclairée à giorno par la pleine
    lune qui voyage avec nous
La Croix du Sud est à l'est et le sud reste tout noir
Il fait une chaleur étouffante

A FINE EVENING

Night falls over the American coast
Not a fish not a bird
A continuous range of uniform mountains all covered
    with lush vegetation
The sea is smooth
The sky too
I think of the two friends I made on board and who
    have just left me in Rio
M. Lopart a stockbroker in Brussels nice charming
    who argued with me during meals or in the evening
    in the smoking room over a bottle of whiskey
And Boubou-blanc-blanc-boubou the best of pals with
    whom I swam for hours in the pool mornings and
    evenings
The three of us made a very jolly group laughing
    ourselves to tears
We annoyed everyone on board scandalized the civil
    servants and the military (ranking officers)
    sent on a mission
I never laughed so much in ten years and laughed
    during twenty days I laughed myself sick and
    gained twelve pounds
Good-bye my good friends see you soon we will meet again on
    board when sailing back to France or some other day in
    Paris or in Brussels or somewhere else in a train that
    will cross the Andes or on board the *Empress* steering
    for Australia we will still have the same barman because
    the world is quite small for such jolly companions
So long so long

AT SEA IN THE DEAD OF NIGHT

The mountainous coast is brilliantly lighted by the full
    moon traveling with us
The Southern Cross is to the east and the south remains
    all dark
It is stifling hot

De gros morceaux de bois nagent dans l'eau opaque
Sur le pont les deux acrobates Allemandes se promènent
    aux trois quarts nues
Elles cherchent de la fraîcheur
Le petit médecin portugais qui accompagne les émi-
    grants de sa nation jusqu'à Buenos-Aires cligne de
    l'œil en passant devant moi
Je le vois s'engouffrer avec les deux Allemandes dans
    une grande cabine inoccupée
Deux navires passent à tribord puis trois à bâbord
Tous les cinq sont éclairés comme pour une fête de nuit
On se croirait dans le port de Monte-Carlo et la forêt
    vierge pousse jusque dans la mer
En dressant l'oreille et en tendant toutes mes facultés
    d'attention j'entends comme le bruissement des
    feuilles
Ou peut-être mon chagrin de quitter le bord demain
Au bout d'un grand quart d'heure je perçois la mince
    chanson d'un émigrant sur le gaillard avant où du linge
    sèche à la lune et me fait des signes

PARIS

Je suis resté toute la nuit sur le pont écoutant les mes-
    sages qui arrivaient par T. S. F. en déchiffrant quel-
    ques bribes
Et les traduisant en clignant des yeux pour les étoiles
Un astre nouveau brillait à la hauteur de mon nez
La braise de mon cigare
Je songeais distraitement à Paris
Et chaque étoile du ciel était remplacée parfois par un
    visage connu
J'ai vu Jean comme une torche follette l'œil malicieux
    d'Erik le regard posé de Fernand et les yeux d'un
    tas de cafés autour de Sanders
Les bésicles rondes d'Eugénia celles de Marcel
Le regard en flèche de Mariette et les yeux dodelinant
    du Gascon

Large pieces of driftwood float in the opaque water
On the deck the two German female acrobats stroll about
   half naked
They are trying to get cool
The little Portuguese doctor who accompanies the emigrants
   from his country to Buenos Aires gives me a wink in
   passing
I see him rush with the two German girls into a vast
   vacant cabin
Two ships sail past to starboard then three to port
All five of them are lit up as for a night festival
You would think you were in Monte Carlo harbor and
   the virgin forest grows into the sea
Ears strained and mind stretched to utmost attention
   it seems I hear the rustling of leaves
Or maybe my sorrow to be leaving the ship tomorrow
After a long quarter of an hour I distinguish the
   tenuous song of an emigrant on the forecastle
   where linen is drying in the moonlight and
   beckons to me

PARIS

I stayed on deck all night long listening to the messages
   that came through on the radio decoding a few snatches
And translating them with a wink to the stars
A new star was shining at the level of my nose
The embers of my cigar
I was absentmindedly thinking of Paris
And each star in the sky turned at times into a familiar
   face
I saw Jean like a sprightly torch the mischievous eyes
   of Erik the poised look of Fernand and the eyes of
   lots of cafés around Sanders*
Eugenia's round specs and those of Marcel
The darting glance of Mariette and the fluttering eyes of the
   fellow from Gascony

De temps en temps Francis et Germaine passaient en
 auto et Abel faisait de la mise en scène et était triste
Puis la T. S. F. reprenait et je regardais les étoiles
Et l'astre nouveau s'allumait à nouveau au bout de
 mon nez
Il m'éclairait comme Raymone
Tout près tout près

AUBE

A l'aube je suis descendu au fond des machines
J'ai écouté pour une dernière fois la respiration profonde
 des pistons
Appuyé à la fragile main-courante de nickel j'ai senti
 pour une dernière fois cette sourde vibration des
 arbres de couche pénétrer en moi avec le relent des
 huiles surchauffées et la tiédeur de la vapeur
Nous avons encore bu un verre le chef mécanicien cet
 homme tranquille et triste qui a un si beau sourire
 d'enfant et qui ne cause jamais et moi
Comme je sortais de chez lui le soleil sortait tout natu-
 rellement de la mer et chauffait déjà dur
Le ciel mauve n'avait pas un nuage
Et comme nous pointions sur Santos notre sillage décri-
 vait un grand arc-de-cercle miroitant sur la mer
 immobile

ILES

Iles
Iles
Iles où l'on ne prendra jamais terre
Iles où l'on ne descendra jamais
Iles couvertes de végétations
Iles tapies comme des jaguars
Iles muettes
Iles immobiles

Now and then Francis and Germaine drove by and Abel was
    staging productions and was sad
Then the broadcasting started again and I watched the stars
And the new star lighted me up again at the tip of my nose
It lighted me up like Raymone
Close close

DAWN

At dawn I went down to the engine room in the bowels
    of the ship
I listened once more for the last time to the deep
    breathing of the pistons
Leaning against the fragile nickel handrail I felt
    once again for the last time that low vibration
    of the power shaft permeate me with the reek
    of overheated oils and tepid warmth of the steam
We had one more drink the chief engineer that quiet
    sad man who has such a beautiful childlike smile
    and never talks and I
As I came out of his room the sun was coming·quite
    naturally out of the sea and was already beating down
    hard
There was not a cloud in the purple sky
And as we were heading for Santos our wake drew a wide
    shimmering bowlike curve on the motionless sea

ISLANDS

Islands
Islands
Islands where one will never land
Islands where one will never go ashore
Islands covered with vegetation
Islands lurking like jaguars
Islands of silence
Islands motionless

Iles inoubliables et sans nom
Je lance mes chaussures par-dessus bord car je voudrais
    bien aller jusqu'à vous

ARRIVÉE A SANTOS

Nous pénétrons entre des montagnes qui se referment
    derrière nous
On ne sait plus où est le large
Voici le pilote qui grimpe l'échelle c'est un métis aux
    grands yeux
Nous entrons dans une baie intérieure qui s'achève par
    un goulet
A gauche il y a une plage éblouissante sur laquelle cir-
    culent des autos à droite la végétation tropicale muette
    dure tombe à la mer comme un niagara de chlorophylle.
Quand on a passé un petit fort portugais riant comme une
    chapelle de la banlieue de Rome et dont les canons
    sont comme des fauteuils où l'on voudrait s'asseoir
    à l'ombre on serpente une heure dans le goulet plein
    d'eau terreuse
Les rives sont basses
Celle de gauche plantée de manguiers et de bambous
    géants autour des bicoques rouges et noires ou bleues
    et noires des nègres
Celle de droite désolée marécageuse pleine de palmiers
    épineux
Le soleil est étourdissant.

A BABORD

Le port
Pas un bruit de machine pas un sifflet pas une sirène
Rien ne bouge on ne voit pas un homme
Aucune fumée monte aucun panache de vapeur
Insolation de tout un port
Il n'y a que le soleil cruel et la chaleur qui tombe du ciel
    et qui monte de l'eau la chaleur éblouissante

Islands unforgettable and nameless
I throw my shoes overboard because I would so much like
   to come to you

ARRIVAL IN SANTOS

We make our way between mountains that close in behind us
You can't tell any more where the open sea is
Here is the pilot climbing up the ladder a half-breed with
   large eyes
We enter an inland bay which ends in narrows
On the left there is a dazzling beach with cars driving
   around on it on the right the silent hard tropical
   vegetation pours into the sea like a chlorophyll
   Niagara Falls
After passing a small Portuguese fort inviting like a
   chapel in the suburbs of Rome and where the cannons
   are like armchairs in which it would be nice to sit
   in the shade we spend an hour meandering through the
   narrows full of muddy water
The banks are low
The left one planted with mango trees and giant bamboos
   around the black and red or black and blue shacks
   of the blacks
The right one deserted marshy full of prickly palms
The sun makes you dizzy

ON PORT SIDE

The harbor
Not a machine humming not a whistle not a foghorn
Nothing stirs not a man in sight
No coils of smoke no puff of steam
The whole harbor suffering from a sunstroke
There is nothing but the harsh sun and the heat falling from
   the sky and rising from the water the dazzling heat

Rien ne bouge
Pourtant il y a là une ville de l'activité une industrie
Vingt-cinq cargos appartenant à dix nations sont à quai
    et chargent du café
Deux cents grues travaillent silencieusement
(A la lorgnette on distingue les sacs de café qui voyagent
    sur les tapis-roulants et les monte-charge continus
La ville est cachée derrière les hangars plats et les grands
    dépôts rectilignes en tôle ondulée)
Rien ne bouge
Nous attendons des heures
Personne ne vient
Aucune barque ne se détache de la rive
Notre paquebot a l'air de se fondre minute par minute
    et de couler lentement dans la chaleur épaisse de se
    gondoler et de couler à pic

A TRIBORD

Une frégate est suspendue en l'air
C'est un oiseau d'une souveraine élégance aux ailes à
    incidence variable et profilées comme un planeur
Deux gros dos squameux émergent de l'eau bourbeuse
    et replongent dans la vase
Des régimes de bananes flottent à vau-l'eau
Depuis que nous sommes là trois nouveaux cargos ont
    surgi derrière nous silencieux et las
La chaleur les écrase

VIE

Le Formose évite sur son ancre et nous virons imper-
    ceptiblement de bord
Une embarcation se détache de la rive
C'est une pirogue taillée dans un tronc d'arbre
Elle est montée par deux petits moricauds
L'un est couché sur le dos immobile

Nothing stirs
Yet there is a town there activity industry
Twenty-five freighters from ten countries are alongside the
    wharf loading coffee
Two hundred cranes work silently
(With binoculars you can see the sacks of coffee traveling
    on conveyor belts and hoists
The town is hidden behind the flat sheds and the large
    rectangular warehouses of corrugated iron)
Nothing stirs
We wait for hours
No one comes
No boat moves off the shore
Our liner seems to melt with every minute and to founder
    slowly into the thickness of the heat to buckle and
    sink straight down

ON STARBOARD

A frigate is hovering in the air
It is a bird of supreme elegance with wings at variable
    angles streamlined like a glider
Two big scaly backs emerge from the miry waters and dive
    back into the mud
Stems of bananas float downstream
Since we arrived three new freighters have loomed up behind
    us silent and weary
Crushed by the heat

LIFE

The *Formosa* swings at anchor and tacks imperceptibly
A craft pulls from the shore
It is a dugout canoe carved from a tree trunk
Steered by two little blackamoors
One is lying on his back motionless

L'autre accroupi à l'avant pagaie nonchalamment
Le soleil joue sur les deux faces de sa pagaie
Ils font lentement le tour du bateau puis retournent à la
    rive

LA PLAGE DE GUARUJA

Il est quatorze heures nous sommes enfin à quai
J'ai découvert un paquet d'hommes à l'ombre dans
    l'ombre ramassée d'une grue
Certificats médicaux passeport douane
Je débarque
Je ne suis pas assis dans l'auto qui m'emporte mais dans
    la chaleur molle épaisse rembourrée comme une
    carrosserie
Mes amis qui m'attendent depuis sept heures du matin
    sur le quai ensoleillé ont encore tout juste la force de
    me serrer la main
Toute la ville retentit de jeunes klaxons qui se saluent
De jeunes klaxons qui nous raniment
De jeunes klaxons qui nous donnent faim
De jeunes klaxons qui nous mènent déjeuner sur la
    plage de Guarujà
Dans un restaurant rempli d'appareils à sous tirs élec-
    triques oiseaux mécaniques appareils automatiques
    qui vous font les lignes de la main gramophones qui
    vous disent la bonne aventure et où l'on mange de la
    bonne vieille cuisine brésilienne savoureuse épicée
    nègre indienne

BANANERAIE

Nous faisons encore un tour en auto avant de prendre
    le train
Nous traversons des bananeraies poussiéreuses
Les abattoirs puants
Une banlieue misérable et une brousse florissante
Puis nous longeons une montagne en terre rouge où
    s'amoncellent des maisons cubiques peinturlurées en
    rouge et en bleu noir des maisons de bois construites

The other squatting at the bow paddles unconcerned
The sun shimmers on both sides of his paddle
They slowly circle around the ship then return to the
    shore

GUARUJÁ BEACH

It is two P.M. we have finally docked
I have discovered a bunch of men in the shade in the
    stocky shade of a crane
Medical certificates passport customs
I go ashore
I am not sitting in the car that takes me but in the
    muggy heavy heat padded like car upholstery
My friends who have been waiting for me since seven A.M.
    on the sun-drenched wharf have barely enough strength
    left to shake hands with me
The whole town resounds with horns tooting youthfully
    to greet one another
Youthful toots that cheer you up
Youthful toots that make you hungry
Youthful toots that take you to lunch on Guarujá Beach
In a restaurant full of slot machines electric shooting
    ranges mechanical birds automatic palm-reading
    machines fortune-telling gramophones and where you
    get good old Brazilian cooking tasty spicy black
    Indian

BANANA PLANTATION

We take another drive in the car before catching the train
We drive through dusty banana plantations
Stinking slaughterhouses
Wretched suburbs and luxuriant bush
Then we skirt a mountain of red earth stacked up with
    cube-shaped houses splashed with red or blue-black paint

sur des placers abandonnés
Deux chèvres naines broutent les plantes rares qui
poussent au bord de la route deux chèvres naines et
un petit cochon bleu

MICTORIO

Le mictorio c'est les W.-C. de la gare
Je regarde toujours cet endroit avec curiosité quand
j'arrive dans un nouveau pays
Les lieux de la gare de Santos sont un petit réduit où
une immense terrine qui me rappelle les grandes jarres
qui sont dans les vignes en Provence où une immense
terrine est enfouie jusqu'au col dans le sol
Un gros boudin de bois noir large et épais est posé en
couronne sur le bord et sert de siège
Cela doit être bien mal commode et trop bas.
C'est exactement le contraire des tinettes de la Bastille
qui elles sont trop haut perchées

LES TINETTES DE LA BASTILLE

Les tinettes de la Bastille servent encore dans les cachots
de la caserne de Reuilly à Paris
Ce sont des pots de grès en forme d'entonnoir renversé
d'environ un mètre trente-cinq de haut
Elles sont au centre des cachots la partie la plus évasée
reposant sur le sol et le petit bout la partie la plus
étroite en l'air
C'est dans cette espèce d'embouchure de trompette qui
est de beaucoup trop haut placée que le soldat puni de
cachot doit réussir à faire ses besoins
Sans rien laisser choir à l'extérieur sinon il rebiffe pour
la même durée de tôle
C'est le supplice de Tantale à rebours
Au début de la guerre j'ai connu des poilus qui pour ce
motif et de vingt-quatre en vingt-quatre heures ont

wooden houses built on deserted placers
Two dwarf goats are grazing the rare plants that grow
   by the roadside two dwarf goats and a little blue pig

MICTORIO

The mictorio is the station's lavatories
I always observe that place with interest when I arrive
   in a new country
The privies in Santos station are a small hovel where
   a huge earthenware pot which reminds me of the large
   jars you see in the vineyards in Provence where a
   huge earthenware pot is buried up to the neck in
   the ground
A big black wood sausage wide and thick crowns the edge
   and makes the seat
It must be sort of uncomfortable and too low
Just the contrary of the tubs at the Bastille which
   are too high up

THE BASTILLE TUBS

The tubs of the Bastille are still used in the cells of the
   Reuilly barracks in Paris
They are stoneware pots shaped like reversed funnels and
   about four feet five high
They are placed in the middle of the cells the wider part on
   the ground and the small end the narrowest part in the air
It is into that kind of trumpet mouthpiece which is set much
   too high that the imprisoned soldier must manage to
   relieve himself
Without dropping anything outside or he doubles his jail
   time
Tantalus's ordeal in reverse
At the beginning of the war I knew privates who for that
   reason from one twenty-four hours to another have spent

passé des mois au cachot puis ils finissaient par passer
au tourniquet comme fortes têtes
On racontait que ces tinettes étaient les anciennes tinettes
de l'ancienne prison de la Bastille

SAO-PAULO RAILWAY C⁰

Le rapide est sous pression
Nous nous installons dans un Pullman pompéien qui
ressemble aux confortables wagons des chemins de fer
égyptiens
Nous sommes autour d'une table de bridge dans de larges
fauteuils d'osier
Il y a un bar au bout du wagon où je bois le premier café
de Santos
Au départ nous croisons un convoi de wagons blancs
qui portent cette inscription
Caloric Cy
Tu parles
J'étouffe

PAYSAGE

La terre est rouge
Le ciel est bleu
La végétation est d'un vert foncé
Ce paysage est cruel dur triste malgré la variété infinie
des formes végétatives
Malgré la grâce penchée des palmiers et les bouquets
éclatants des grands arbres en fleurs fleurs de carême

DANS LE TRAIN

Le train va assez vite
Les signaux aiguilles et passages à niveau fonctionnent
comme en Angleterre
La nature est d'un vert beaucoup plus foncé que chez
nous
Cuivrée

months in jail then were finally court-martialed for being
strongheaded
The story went that these tubs were the old tubs of the
old prison of the Bastille

SÃO PAULO RAILWAY CO.

The express is under steam
We settle into a Pompeian Pullman car which looks like the
comfortable Egyptian coaches
We are sitting around a bridge table in wide wicker
armchairs
There is a bar at the end of the car where I have the
first Santos coffee
As we go we pass a train of white cars on which you
read
Caloric Co
You bet
I am suffocating

LANDSCAPE

Red earth
Blue sky
Dark-green vegetation
Cruel hard sad landscape in spite of the infinite variety
of vegetative forms
In spite of the graceful curve of palm trees and the vivid
clusters of tall trees in bloom Lenten flowers

ON THE TRAIN

The train goes pretty fast
The signals switches and level crossings work as they do
in England
Nature is a much darker green than at home
Copper colored

Fermée
La forêt a un visage d'indien
Tandis que le jaune et le blanc dominent dans nos prés
Ici c'est le bleu céleste qui colore les campos fleuris

PARANAPIAÇABA

Le Paranapiaçaba est la Serra do Mar
C'est ici que le train est hissé par des câbles et franchit
    la dure montagne en plusieurs sections
Toutes les stations sont suspendues dans le vide
Il y a beaucoup de chutes d'eau et il a fallu entreprendre
    de grands travaux d'art pour étayer partout la mon-
    tagne qui s'effrite
Car la Serra est une montagne pourrie comme les Rognes
    au-dessus de Bionnasay mais les Rognes couvertes de
    forêts tropicales
Les mauvaises herbes qui poussent sur les talus dans la
    tranchée entre les voies sont toutes des plantes rares
    qu'on ne voit à Paris que dans les vitrines des grands
    horticulteurs
Dans une gare trois métis indolents étaient en train de
    les sarcler

LIGNE TÉLÉGRAPHIQUE

Vous voyez cette ligne télégraphique au fond de la vallée
    et dont le tracé rectiligne coupe la forêt sur la mon-
    tagne d'en face
Tous les poteaux en sont de fer
Quand on l'a installée les poteaux étaient en bois
Au bout de trois mois il leur poussait des branches
On les a alors arrachés retournés et replantés la tête en
    bas les racines en l'air
Au bout de trois mois il leur repoussait de nouvelles
    branches ils reprenaient racine et recommençaient à
    vivre
Il fallut tout arracher et pour rétablir une nouvelle ligne
    faire venir à grands frais des poteaux de fer de Pitts-
    burg

Closed in
The forest has the face of an Indian
Whereas yellow and white predominate in our meadows
Here celestial blue colors the flowering campos

PARANAPIACABA

The Serra Paranapiacaba is the Serra do Mar
That's where the train is hoisted by cables and crosses
    the looming mountain in several sections
All the stations are hanging in the air
There are lots of waterfalls and big artful constructions
    had to be undertaken to support the crumbling mountain
    everywhere
For the Serra is a rotten mountain like the Rognes above
    Bionnasay but the Rognes covered with tropical forests
The weeds growing on the slopes of the ditch between the
    tracks are all rare plants which you see in Paris only in
    the shopwindows of the leading horticulturists
In a railway station three indolent half-breeds are pulling
    the weeds

TELEGRAPH LINE

You see that telegraph line at the bottom of the valley
    cutting straight through the forest on the opposite
    mountain
All the poles are made of iron
When it was first set up the poles were wooden
Three months later branches were growing out of them
Then they were pulled out turned upside down replanted
    head down roots in the air
Three months later new branches were growing again they
    were taking root again and starting a new life
Everything had to be pulled out and to set up a new line
    costly iron poles had to be brought in from Pittsburgh

TROUÉES

Échappées sur la mer
Chutes d'eau
Arbres chevelus moussus
Lourdes feuilles caoutchoutées luisantes
Un vernis de soleil
Une chaleur bien astiquée
Reluisance
Je n'écoute plus la conversation animée de mes amis qui
    se partagent les nouvelles que j'ai apportées de Paris
Des deux côtés du train toute proche ou alors de l'autre
    côté de la vallée lointaine
La forêt est là et me regarde et m'inquiète et m'attire
    comme le masque d'une momie
Je regarde
Pas l'ombre d'un œil

VISAGE RAVINÉ

Il y a les frondaisons de la forêt les frondaisons
Cette architecture penchée ouvragée comme la façade
    d'une cathédrale avec des niches et des enjolivures
    des masses perpendiculaires et des fûts frêles

PIRATININGA

Quand on franchit la crête de la Serra et qu'on est sorti
    des brouillards qui l'encapuchonnent le pays devient
    moins inégal
Il finit par n'être plus qu'un vaste plateau ondulé borné
    au nord par des montagnes bleues
La terre est rouge
Ce plateau offre des petits bouquets de bois peu élevés
    d'une étendue peu considérable très rapprochés les
    uns des autres qui souvent se touchent par quelque
    point et sont disséminés au milieu d'une pelouse pres-
    que rase

CLEARINGS

Vistas on the sea
Waterfalls
Hairy mossy trees
Heavy rubbery shiny leaves
Sun polish
Well-furbished heat
Gloss
I no longer listen to the lively conversation of my friends
    who share with one another the news I brought from Paris
On both sides of the train very near or on the other side of
    the distant valley
There is the forest which looks at me and disturbs me and
    entices me like the mask of a mummy
I look out
Not an eye

FURROWED FACE

There is the greenery of the forest the greenery
That slanting architecture wrought like a cathedral front
    with recesses embellishments perpendicular masses
    and slender shafts

PIRATININGA

When you cross over the ridge of the Serra and are above the
    fogs that wrap it up as in a hood the landscape is less
    uneven
It finally is nothing more than a vast undulating plateau
    bounded on the north by blue mountains
The earth is red
On the plateau there are small clusters of low groves
    covering little ground very close to one another often
    joining at the edges and scattered in the middle of an
    almost bare lawn

Il est difficile de déterminer s'il y a plus de terrain cou-
   vert de bois qu'il n'y en a de pâturages
Cela fait une sorte de marqueterie de deux nuances de
   vert bien différentes et bien tranchées
Celle de l'herbe d'une couleur tendre
Celle des bois d'une teinte foncée

BOTANIQUE

L'araucaria attire les regards
On admire sa taille gigantesque
Et surtout ses branches
Qui nées à différentes hauteurs
s'élèvent en manière de candélabre
Et s'arrêtent toutes au même niveau pour former un
   plateau parfaitement égal
On voit aussi le grand seneçon aux fleurs d'un jaune d'or
   les myrtées
Les térébinthacées
La composée si commune qu'on nomme Alecrim do
   campo le romarin des champs
Et le petit arbre à feuilles ternées n° 1204 bis
Mais mon plus grand bonheur est de ne pas pouvoir
   mettre de nom sur des tas de plantes toutes plus belles
   les unes que les autres
Et que je ne connais pas
Et que je vois pour la première fois
Et que j'admire

IGNORANCE

Je n'écoute plus toutes les belles histoires que l'on me
   raconte sur l'avenir le passé le présent du Brésil
Je vois par la portière du train qui maintenant accélère
   sa marche
La grande fougère ptéris caudata
Qu'il n'y a pas un oiseau
Les grandes fourmilières maçonnées

It is difficult to determine whether more ground is
   covered with groves than with pastures
It is like an inlaid work of two quite different and
   contrasting shades of green
The grass in a soft shade
The groves in a dark tone

BOTANY

The araucaria draws attention
People admire its gigantic size
And especially its branches
Which sprouting at different heights
Rise like the branches of a candelabrum
And stop all at the same level forming a perfectly even platform
You can also see the big groundsel tree with yellow flowers
   the myrtle
The turpentine tree
The so common composite called Alecrim do campo the
   field rosemary
And the small tree with trifoliate leaves number 1204 bis
But my greatest happiness is to be unable to put a name
   on lots of plants each one more beautiful than the other
And which I don't know
And which I see for the first time
And which I admire

IGNORANCE

I no longer listen to all the beautiful stories I am told on
   the future the past the present of Brazil
Through the door of the train which is now taking on speed
   I see
The tall fern *Pteris caudata*
That there is not a bird
The big masonry anthills

Que les lys forment ici des buissons impénétrables
Les savanes se composent tantôt d'herbes sèches et de
sous-arbrisseaux tantôt au milieu des herbes d'arbres
épars çà et là presque toujours tortueux et rabougris
Que les ricins atteignent plusieurs mètres de hauteur
Il y a quelques animaux dans les prés des bœufs à
longues cornes des chevaux maigres à allure de mus-
tang et des taureaux zébus
Qu'il n'y a aucune trace de culture
Puis je ne sais plus rien de tout ce que je vois
Des formes
Des formes de végétation
Des palmiers des cactus on ne sait plus comment appeler
ça des manches à balai surmontés d'aigrettes roses il
paraît que c'est un fruit aphrodisiaque

SAO-PAULO

Enfin voici des usines une banlieue un gentil petit
tramway
Des conduites électriques
Une rue populeuse avec des gens qui vont faire leurs
emplettes du soir
Un gazomètre
Enfin on entre en gare
Saint-Paul
Je crois être en gare de Nice
Ou débarquer à Charring-Cross à Londres
Je trouve tous mes amis
Bonjour
C'est moi

Le Havre-Saint-Paul, février 1924.

That here the lilies grow into impenetrable bushes
The savannas are now dry grass and underbrush now trees
    scattered here and there through the grass almost
    always twisted and stunted
That the castor oil plants grow several yards high
There are some cattle in the fields long-horned steers
    skinny horses that look like mustangs and zebu bulls
That there is no trace of culture
Then I no longer know anything about all I see
Forms
Forms of vegetation
Palm tree cactus one does not know what to call it
    a broomstick with pink tufts it is supposed to be
    an aphrodisiac fruit

SÃO PAULO

At last factories suburbs a nice little trolley
Electric wires
A crowded street with people out for their evening shopping
A gasholder
Finally we pull into the station
São Paulo
I think I am in the Nice station
Or arriving at Charing Cross in London
I find all my friends
Hi
Here I am

                          Le Havre–São Paulo, February 1924.

II. SAO-PAULO

DEBOUT

La nuit s'avance
Le jour commence à poindre
Une fenêtre s'ouvre
Un homme se penche au dehors en fredonnant
Il est en bras de chemise et regarde de par le monde
Le vent murmure doucement comme une tête bour-
    donnante

LA VILLE SE RÉVEILLE

Les premiers trams ouvriers passent
Un homme vend des journaux au milieu de la place
Il se démène dans les grandes feuilles de papier qui bat-
    tent des ailes et exécute une espèce de ballet à lui tout
    seul tout en s'accompagnant de cris gutturaux...
        STADO...ERCIO...EIO
Des klaxons lui répondent
Et les premières autos passent à toute vitesse

KLAXONS ÉLECTRIQUES

Ici on ne connaît pas la Ligue du Silence
Comme dans tous les pays neufs
La joie de vivre et de gagner de l'argent s'exprime par la
    voix des klaxons et la pétarade des pots d'échappement
    ouverts

MENU FRETIN

Le ciel est d'un bleu cru
Le mur d'en face est d'un blanc cru
Le soleil cru me tape sur la tête

II. SÃO PAULO

GETTING UP

Night draws to an end
Day starts to break
A window opens
A man leans out humming a tune
He is in shirt sleeves and looks about the world
The wind sighs softly like a buzzing head

THE CITY WAKES UP

The first workmen's trolleys go by
A man sells newspapers in the middle of the square
He struggles with the large sheets of paper flapping
   their wings and performs a kind of solo ballet
   accompanying himself with guttural calls
   STADO . . . ERCIO . . . EIO
Horns answer him
And the first cars speed by

ELECTRIC HORNS

Here the league of silence is unknown
As in all new countries
The joy of living and making money is expressed through
   tooting horns and roaring open mufflers

SMALL FRY

Harsh blue sky
Harsh white wall across the street
Harsh sun beating down on my head

Une négresse installée sur une petite terrasse fait frire de
  tout petits poissons sur un réchaud découpé dans une
  vieille boîte à biscuits
Deux négrillons rongent une tige de canne à sucre

PAYSAGE

Le mur ripoliné de la PENSION MILANESE s'encadre
  dans ma fenêtre
Je vois une tranche de l'avenue Sao-João
Trams autos trams
Trams-trams trams trams
Des mulets jaunes attelés par trois tirent de toutes petites
  charrettes vides
Au-dessus des poivriers de l'avenue se détache l'enseigne
  géante de la CASA TOKIO
Le soleil verse du vernis

SAINT-PAUL

J'adore cette ville
Saint-Paul est selon mon cœur
Ici nulle tradition
Aucun préjugé
Ni ancien ni moderne
Seuls comptent cet appétit furieux cette confiance absolue
  cet optimisme cette audace ce travail ce labeur cette
  spéculation qui font construire dix maisons par heure
  de tous styles ridicules grotesques beaux grands petits
  nord sud égyptien yankee cubiste
Sans autre préoccupation que de suivre les statistiques
  prévoir l'avenir le confort l'utilité la plus-value et
  d'attirer une grosse immigration
Tous les pays
Tous les peuples
J'aime ça
Les deux trois vieilles maisons portugaises qui restent
  sont des faïences bleues

A black woman on a small terrace is frying tiny little
   fish on a portable stove cut out of an old biscuit tin
Two pickaninnies chew a sugarcane stem

LANDSCAPE

The wall of the PENSION MILANESE painted in enamel gloss
   is framed in my window
I see a section of São João Avenue
Trams cars trams
Tram-trams trams trams
Yellow mules harnessed in teams of three draw tiny
   empty carts
Above the avenue's pepper trees stands out the gigantic sign
   of CASA TOKYO
The sun pours varnish

SÃO PAULO

I adore this city
São Paulo is a place after my own heart
No tradition here
No prejudice
Whether old or new
Nothing matters but that furious greed that absolute
   confidence that optimism that daring that work
   that toil that speculation which have ten houses
   built per hour in every style ridiculous grotesque
   beautiful big small northern southern Egyptian
   Yankee cubist
With no other concern but keeping up with statistics
   foreseeing the future the comfort the utility
   the increase in value and attracting a large
   number of immigrants
All countries
All nations
I love that
The two three old Portuguese houses left are pieces of
   blue china

III.

DÉPART

Pour la dernière fois je reprends le caminho do Mar
Mais je n'en jouis pas à cause d'Oswald qui a le cafard
Et qui fait le sombre ténébreux
La Serra est dans le brouillard
L'auto a des à-coups
Le moteur des ratés

A QUAI

Au revoir mes bons amis Au revoir
Rentrez vite à São-Paulo avant la nuit
On parle une dernière fois des mitrailleuses de la révolu-
tion
Moi je reste seul à bord de ce grand bateau hollandais
plein d'Allemands de Hollandais d'Argentins enfantins
brillants cosmétiqués et de 2-3 faux Anglais
Les émigrants espagnols rentrent dans leur pays
Ils ont gagné un peu d'argent puisqu'ils peuvent se payer
un billet de retour et ils ont l'air bien content
Un couple danse au son d'un accordéon
C'est encore une jota

CABINE 2

C'est la mienne
Elle est toute blanche
J'y serai très bien
Tout seul
Car il me faut beaucoup travailler
Pour rattraper les 9 mois au soleil
Les 9 mois au Brésil
Les 9 mois aux Amis

III

DEPARTURE

For the last time I take again the camiño do Mar
But I don't enjoy it because of Oswald who is down in
    the dumps
And acts a romantic hero in somber gloom
The Serra is wrapped in fog
The car is misbehaving
The engine is misfiring

AT THE QUAY

Farewell my good friends farewell
Get quickly back to São Paulo before dark
We talk for a last time of the machine guns the revolution
I stay alone on board this large Dutch ship
    full of Germans Dutch Argentinians childish shiny
    caked with cosmetics and 2-3 fake Englishmen
The Spanish emigrants return home
They have made some money since they can afford a return
    fare and they look quite pleased
A couple dances to the tune of an accordion
It is again a jota

CABIN 2

It's mine
It is all white
I'll be fine here
All by myself
For I have to work a lot
To make up for the 9 months in the sun
The 9 months in Brazil
The 9 months given up to friends

Et je dois travailler pour Paris
C'est pourquoi j'aime déjà ce bateau archibondé où je ne
    vois personne avec qui faire causette

A TABLE

J'ai donné un bon pourboire au maître d'hôtel pour avoir
    dans un coin une petite table à moi tout seul
Je ne ferai pas de connaissances
Je regarde les autres et je mange
Voici le premier menu de goût européen
J'avoue que je mange avec plaisir ces plats d'Europe
Potage Pompadour
Culotte de bœuf à la bruxelloise
Perdreau sur canapé
Le goût est le sens le plus atavique le plus réactionnaire
    le plus national
Analytique
Aux antipodes de l'amour du toucher du toucher de
    l'amour en pleine évolution et croissance universelle
Révolutionnaire
Synthétique

RETARD

Il est près de deux heures du matin et nous ne partons
    toujours pas
On n'arrête pas d'embarquer du café
Les sacs vont vont et vont sur les monte-charge continus
    et tombent à fond de cale comme les porcs gonflés de
    Chicago
J'en ai marre
Je vais me coucher

And I must work for Paris
That's why I already love this overcrowded ship
    where I don't see anyone to chat with

DINNER TIME

I gave a large tip to the chief steward in order to have
    a small table in a corner to myself
I am not going to meet anyone
I look at the others and eat
That's the first European-style menu
I must admit that I eat these dishes from Europe with
    pleasure
Pompadour consommé
Beef tenderloin Brussels
Partridge on toast
Taste is the most atavistic sense the most reactionary
    the most national
Analytical
Diametrically opposed to the love of touch to the touch
    of love in full development and universal growth
Revolutionary
Synthetic

DELAY

It's almost two A.M. and we are still here
They keep loading coffee
The sacks go go and go on the conveyor belts
    and drop down into the hold like the swollen
    hogs in Chicago
I am fed up
I am going to bed

RÉVEIL

Je suis nu
J'ai déjà pris mon bain
Je me frictionne à l'eau de Cologne
Un voilier lourdement secoué passe dans mon hublot
Il fait froid ce matin
Il y a de la brume
Je range mes papiers
J'établis un horaire
Mes journées seront bien remplies
Je n'ai pas une minute à perdre
J'écris

LA BRISE

Pas un bruit pas une secousse
Le « Gelria » tient admirablement la mer
Sur ce paquebot de luxe avec ses orchestres tziganes dans
    chaque cache-pot on se lève tard
La matinée m'appartient
Mes manuscrits sont étalés sur ma couchette
La brise les feuillette d'un doigt distrait
Présences

RIO DE JANEIRO

Une lumière éclatante inonde l'atmosphère
Une lumière si colorée et si fluide que les objets qu'elle
    touche
Les rochers roses
Le phare blanc qui les surmonte
Les signaux du sémaphore en semblent liquéfiés
Et voici maintenant que je sais le nom des montagnes qui
    entourent cette baie merveilleuse
Le Géant couché
La Gavéa
Le Bico de Papagaio

WAKING UP

I am naked
I have already had my bath
I rub myself with eau de cologne
A roughly tossed sailing ship goes by my porthole
It is cold this morning
It is misty
I put my papers in order
I set up a timetable
My days will be full
I don't have a minute to waste
I write

BREEZE

Not a sound no tossing
The *Gelria* is an admirable sailer
On board this luxury liner with its Hungarian gypsy
    orchestras in every flower box people get up late
The morning is mine
My manuscripts are spread out on my berth
The breeze fingers through them absentmindedly
Presences

RIO DE JANEIRO

A dazzling light floods the air
A light so rich in color and so fluid that the objects
    it touches upon
The pink rocks
The white lighthouses standing over them
The semaphore signals all seem liquefied by it
And now I know the names of the mountains that
    circle this marvelous bay
The Sleeping Giant
The Gavea
Bico de Papagaio

Le Corcovado
Le Pain de Sucre que les compagnons de Jean de Léry
  appelaient le Pot de Beurre
Et les aiguilles étranges de la chaîne des Orgues
Bonjour Vous

DINER EN VILLE

Mr. Lopart n'était plus à Rio il était parti samedi par le
  « Lutetia »
J'ai dîné en ville avec le nouveau directeur
Après avoir signé le contrat de 24 F/N type Grand Sport
  je l'ai mené dans un petit caboulot sur le port
Nous avons mangé des crevettes grillées
Des langues de dorade à la mayonnaise
Du tatou
(La viande de tatou a le goût de la viande de renne chère
  à Satie)
Des fruits du pays mamans bananes oranges de Bahia
Chacun a bu son fiasco de chianti

LE MATIN M'APPARTIENT

Le soleil se lève à six heures moins le quart
Le vent a beaucoup fraîchi
Le matin le pont m'appartient jusqu'à 9 heures
Je regarde les matelots qui épongent le spardeck
Les hautes vagues
Un vapeur brésilien que nous rattrapons
Un seul et unique oiseau blanc et noir
Quand apparaissent les premières femmes que le vent
  secoue et les fillettes qu'il trousse en découvrant leur
  petit derrière en chair de poule je redescends dans ma
  cabine
Et me remets au travail

Corvocado
The Sugar Loaf which Jean de Léry's companions
    used to call the Butter Jar
And the strange needles of the Organ Range
Hello You

DINING IN TOWN

M. Lopart was no longer in Rio he had left Saturday
    on the *Lutetia*
I had dinner in town with the new director
After signing a contract for 24 F/N Grand Sport
    I took him to a small harbor pub
We had broiled shrimps
Sea bream tongues with mayonnaise
Armadillo
    (Armadillo meat tastes like reindeer meat which Satie
    likes so much)
Local fruit mammees bananas Bahia oranges
Each one drank a flask of Chianti

MORNINGS ARE MINE

The sun rises at a quarter to six
The wind is much cooler
In the morning I have the deck to myself until 9 o'clock
I watch the sailors mopping the spar deck
The high waves
A Brazilian steamer we catch up with
A single solitary black and white bird
When the first women appear tossed about by the wind
    and the little girls with their skirts blown up
    uncovering their goose-fleshed little buttocks
    I return to my cabin
And get back to work

ÉCRIRE

Ma machine bat en cadence
Elle sonne au bout de chaque ligne
Les engrenages grasseyent
De temps en temps je me renverse dans mon fauteuil de
    jonc et je lâche une grosse bouffée de fumée
Ma cigarette est toujours allumée
J'entends alors le bruit des vagues
Les gargouillements de l'eau étranglée dans la tuyauterie
du lavabo
Je me lève et trempe ma main dans l'eau froide
Ou je me parfume
J'ai voilé le miroir de l'armoire à glace pour ne pas me
    voir écrire
Le hublot est une rondelle de soleil
Quand je pense
Il résonne comme la peau d'un tambour et parle fort

MAUVAISE FOI

Ce sacré maître d'hôtel à qui j'avais tout de même donné
    un bon pourboire pour être seul vient me trouver avec
    son air de chat miteux
Il me prie de la part du commandant de venir prendre
    place à la table d'honneur
Je suis furieux mais ne puis refuser
Au dîner il se trouve que le commandant est un homme
    très sympathique
Je suis entre un attaché d'ambassade à La Haye et un
    consul anglais à Stockholm
De l'autre côté il y a une sommité mondiale en bacté-
    riologie et son épouse qui est une femme douce et
    gourmande toute blanche de peau avec des yeux ronds
    et mats
Mes paradoxes antimusicaux et mes théories culinaires
    secouent la table d'indignation
L'attaché à La Haye trempe son monocle dans le bouillon
Le consul à Stockholm devient vert-congestion comme
    un pyjama rayé

WRITING

My typewriter has a rhythmical clank
It rings at the end of each line
The gearings burr
Now and then I lean back in my wicker armchair
   and blow a big puff of smoke
My cigarette is always lit
Then I hear the sound of the waves
The gurgling of the water compressed in the washbasin
   pipes
I get up and dip my hand in cold water
Or put some perfume on
I have veiled the mirror of the wardrobe so as not to see
   myself writing
The porthole is a round slice of sun
When I think
It resounds like a drumhead and speaks loudly

BAD FAITH

That damned chief steward whom I did after all tip
   generously to be left alone comes to me with that seedy
   cat's look
He invites me on behalf of the captain to sit at the head table
I am furious but I can't say no
At dinner it turns out that the captain is a very pleasant
   fellow
I am sitting between an embassy attaché at The Hague and
   an English consul in Stockholm
Across from me is a world authority in bacteriology and his
   wife who is a sweet and greedy woman with a very
   white skin and round opaque eyes
My antimusical paradoxes and my culinary theories shake
   the table with indignation
The attaché from The Hague dips his eyeglass in the broth
The Stockholm consul turns green and congested like
   striped pajamas

La sommité bactériologique allonge encore sa tête poin-
tue de furet
Son épouse glousse et se ride du centre vers la périphérie
si bien que tout son visage finit par ressembler à un
nombril de poussah
Le commandant cligne de l'œil avec malice

SMOKING

Il n'y a que les miteux qui n'ont pas de smoking à bord
Il n'y a que les gens trop bien élevés qui ont des smokings
à bord
Je mets un petit complet en cheviotte d'Angleterre et la
mer est d'un bleu aussi uni que mon complet bleu
tropical

LA NUIT MONTE

J'ai bien observé comment cela se passait
Quand le soleil est couché
C'est la mer qui s'assombrit
Le ciel conserve encore longtemps une grande clarté
La nuit monte de l'eau et encercle lentement tout l'hori-
zon
Puis le ciel s'assombrit à son tour avec lenteur
Il y a un moment où il fait tout noir
Puis le noir de l'eau et le noir du ciel reculent
Il s'établit une transparence éburnéenne avec des reflets
dans l'eau et des poches obscures au ciel
Puis le Sac à Charbon sous la Croix du Sud
Puis la Voie Lactée

The bacteriology authority pulls an even longer pointed
   ferret's face
His wife chuckles and her face shrivels up from its center
   to the periphery so that the whole of it finally looks
   like the navel of a potbellied Chinese idol
The captain winks slyly

TUXEDO

Only the seedy have no tuxedo on board
Only those who are too well bred have tuxedos on board
I put on a nice little English Cheviot suit and the sea
   is as evenly blue as my tropical blue suit

NIGHT RISES

I have watched carefully how it happened
When the sun has set
The sea darkens
The sky remains quite light for a long time
The night rises from the water and slowly encircles
   the whole horizon
Then in turn the sky darkens slowly
For a while it is pitch black
Then the black of the water and the black of the sky
   recede
An eburnean transparency settles in with reflections
   on the water and dark pockets in the sky
Then the Coalsack under the Southern Cross*
Then the Milky Way

TRAVERSÉE SANS HISTOIRE

Hollande Hollande Hollande
Fumée plein le fumoir
Tziganes plein l'orchestre
Fauteuils plein le salon
Familles familles familles
Trous plein les bas
Et les femmes qui tricotent qui tricotent

CHALEUR

De La Plata à Pernambouc il y a six jours en transatlan-
    tique rapide
On voit souvent la côte mais pas un seul oiseau
Comme à l'intérieur de l'immense État de Saint-Paul on
    reste des jours entiers à rouler sur les routes dans la
    poussière
Sans faire lever un seul oiseau
Tant il fait chaud

CAP FRIE

J'ai entendu cette nuit une voix d'enfant derrière ma
    porte
Douce
Modulée
Pure
Ça m'a fait du bien

INCOGNITO DÉVOILÉ

Voici déjà quelques jours que j'intriguais énormément
    mes compagnons de table
Ils se demandaient ce que je pouvais bien être
Je parlais bactériologie avec la sommité mondiale
Femmes et boîtes de nuit avec le commandant
Théories kantiennes de la paix avec l'attaché à La Haye

CAREFREE CROSSING

Holland Holland Holland
Smoke all over the smoking room
Hungarian gypsies all over the orchestra
Armchairs all over the lounge
Families families families
Holes all over the stockings
And the women knitting knitting

HEAT

From La Plata to Pernambuco it takes six days in a
    fast transatlantic liner
You often see the coast but not a single bird
As inland in the huge state of São Paulo you spend
    days driving on the roads in the dust
Without startling a single bird
It is that hot

CAPE FRIO

I heard a child's voice behind my door last night
Soft
Modulated
Pure
It made me feel good

UNMASKED INCOGNITO

For quite a few days I have been an intriguing puzzle
    to my tablemates
They have been wondering what on earth I could be
I talked bacteriology with the world authority
Women and nightclubs with the captain
Kantian theories of peace with the attaché from The Hague

Affaires de fret avec le consul anglais
Paris cinéma musique banque vitalisme aviation
Ce soir à table comme je lui faisais un compliment la
    femme de la sommité mondiale dit C'est vrai
Monsieur est poète
Patatras
Elle l'a appris de la femme du jockey qui est en deuxième
Je ne puis pas lui en vouloir car son sourire en forme de
    nombril gourmand m'amuse plus que tout au monde
Je voudrais bien savoir comment elle arrive à si bien
    plisser un visage grassouillet et rond

NOURRICES ET SPORTS

Il y a plusieurs nourrices à bord
Des sèches et des pas sèches
Quand on joue aux palets sur le pont
Chaque fois que la jeune Allemande se penche elle
    montre deux petits seins blottis au fond de son corsage
Tous les hommes du passager des premières aux matelots
    connaissent ce jeu et tous passent par le pont babord
    pour voir ces deux choses rondes au nid
On doit en parler jusque dans la cambuse
Au bout d'un banc
Dans un coin sombre
Un nourrisson se pend et fait gicler un grand sein de
    négresse abondant et gommeux comme un régime de
    bananes

VIE DANGEREUSE

Aujourd'hui je suis peut-être l'homme le plus heureux du
    monde
Je possède tout ce que je ne désire pas
Et la seule chose à laquelle je tienne dans la vie chaque
    tour de l'hélice m'en rapproche
Et j'aurai peut-être tout perdu en arrivant

Freight problems with the English consul
Paris movies music bank vitalism flying
Tonight at dinner while I was paying her a compliment
   the world authority's wife said it's true
He is a poet
Bang
She heard it from the jockey's wife who is in tourist class
I can't blame her since I have more fun with her greedy
   navel-shaped smile than with anything else in the world
I would really like to know how she manages to wrinkle
   up a round plumpish face so well

WET NURSES AND SPORTS

There are several nurses on board
Dry and wet ones
When we play quoits on deck
Each time the young German leans forward she shows
   two small breasts nestling in her blouse
All the men from first-class passengers to deckhands
   know that game and they all walk across
   the portside deck to see these two round things
   in their nest
It must be talked about as far down as the steward's room
At the end of a bench
In a dark corner
A baby pulls on the large breast of a black woman and makes
   it spurt out plentiful and sticky like a bunch of bananas

DANGEROUS LIVING

Today I am perhaps the happiest man in the world
I own all that I don't desire
And the only thing that matters to me in life comes
   closer to me with each turn of the propeller
And perhaps I'll have lost everything when I arrive

COQUILLES

Les fautes d'orthographe et les coquilles font mon
    bonheur
Il y a des jours où j'en ferais exprès
C'est tricher
J'aime beaucoup les fautes de prononciation les hésita-
    tions de la langue et l'accent de tous les terroirs

UN JOUR VIENDRA

Un jour viendra
La technique moderne n'y suffit plus
Chaque traversée coûte un million aux électeurs
Avec les avions et les dirigeables cela coûtera dix millions
Les câbles sous-marins ma cabine de luxe les roues les
    travaux des ports les grandes industries mangent de
    l'argent
Toute cette activité prodigieuse qui fait notre orgueil
Les machines n'y suffisent plus
Faillite
Sur son fumier Job se sert encore de son face-massage
    électrique
C'est gai

COUCHER DE SOLEIL

Nous sommes en vue des côtes
Le coucher de soleil a été extraordinaire
Dans le flamboiement du soir
D'énormes nuages perpendiculaires et d'une hauteur folle
Chimères griffons et une grande victoire ailée sont restés
    toute la nuit au-dessus de l'horizon
Au petit jour tout le troupeau se trouvait réuni jaune et
    rose au-dessus de Bahia en damier

MISPRINTS

Spelling mistakes and misprints delight me
Some days I feel like making some on purpose
That's cheating
I am very fond of mistakes in pronunciation speech
    hesitations and all local accents

THE DAY WILL COME

The day will come
Modern technology can no longer cope
Each crossing costs the taxpayers a million
With the planes and the airships that will cost ten million
The submarine cables my luxury cabin the wheels the harbor
    constructions the big manufacturers eat up the money
All that prodigious activity we take pride in
The machines can't cope any more
Bankruptcy
On his dunghill Job is still using his electric facial massage
It is not funny

SUNSET

The coastline is within sight
The sunset has been extraordinary
In the evening ablaze
Huge clouds perpendicular and wildly high
Chimeras griffins and a tall winged victory have stayed
    all night high-edging the horizon
At dawn they all come together in a herd yellow
    and pink above the Bahia checkerboard

BAHIA

Lagunes églises palmiers maisons cubiques
Grandes barques avec deux voiles rectangulaires renver-
    sées qui ressemblent aux jambes immenses d'un pan-
    talon que le vent gonfle
Petites barquettes à aileron de requin qui bondissent entre
    les lames de fond
Grands nuages perpendiculaires renflés colorés comme
    des poteries
Jaunes et bleues

HIC HAEC HOC

J'ai acheté trois ouistitis que j'ai baptisés Hic Haec Hoc
Douze colibris
Mille cigares
Et une main de bahiana grande comme un pied
Avec ça j'emporte le souvenir du plus bel éclat de rire

PERNAMBOUCO

Victor Hugo l'appelle Fernandbouc aux Montagnes
    Bleues
Et un vieil auteur que je lis Ferdinandbourg aux mille
    Églises
En indien ce nom signifie la Bouche Fendue
Voici ce que l'on voit aujourd'hui quand on arrive du
    large et que l'on fait une escale d'une heure et demie
Des terres basses sablonneuses
Une jetée en béton armé et une toute petite grue
Une deuxième jetée en béton armé et une immense grue
Une troisième jetée en béton armé sur laquelle on édifie
    des hangars en béton armé
Quelques cargos à quai
Une longue suite de baraques numérotées
Et par-derrière quelques coupoles deux trois clochers et
    un observatoire astronomique

BAHIA

Lagoons churches palm trees cubelike houses
Large boats with two rectangular sails blown back
    which resemble huge pant legs puffed up by the wind
Small craft shark-finned which leap and bound
    in the billows
Large perpendicular clouds potbellied painted like
    ceramics
Yellow and blue

HIC HAEC HOC

I bought three marmosets and named them Hic Haec Hoc
Twelve hummingbirds
A thousand cigars
And a Bahian hand as large as a foot
With this I take with me the memory of the most beautiful
    peal of laughter

PERNAMBUCO

Victor Hugo calls it Fernandbouc of the Blue Mountains
And an old author I am reading Ferdinandbourg of a
    thousand churches
In Indian that name means Slit Mouth
Here is what you see today when you arrive from the
    open sea and put in for an hour and a half
Low sandy lands
A concrete pier and a tiny crane
A second concrete pier and a huge crane
A third concrete pier on which concrete warehouses
    are being built
Some docked freighters
A long series of numbered shanties
And behind a few cupolas two or three steeples and an
    astronomical observatory

Il y a également les tanks de l' « American Petroleum C⁰ »
et de la « Caloric »
Du soleil de la chaleur et de la tôle ondulée

ADRIENNE LECOUVREUR ET COCTEAU

J'ai encore acheté deux tout petits ouistitis
Et deux oiseaux avec des plumes comme en papier moiré
Mes petits singes ont des boucles d'oreilles
Mes oiseaux ont les ongles dorés
J'ai baptisé le plus petit singe Adrienne Lecouvreur
     l'autre Jean
J'ai donné un oiseau à la fille de l'amiral argentin qui est
     à bord
C'est une jeune fille bête et qui louche des deux yeux
Elle donne un bain de pied à son oiseau pour lui dédorer
     les pattes
L'autre chante dans ma cabine dans quelques jours il
     imitera tous les bruits familiers et sonnera comme ma
     machine à écrire
Quand j'écris mes petits singes me regardent
Je les amuse beaucoup
Ils s'imaginent qu'ils me tiennent en cage

CHALEUR

Je meurs de chaleur dans ma cabine et je ne puis pas
     aérer pour ne pas exposer ma petite famille de petites
     bêtes au courant d'air
Tant pis
Je reste dans ma cabine
J'étouffe et j'écris j'écris
J'écris pour leur faire plaisir
Ces petites bêtes sont bien gentilles et moi aussi

There are also the tankers of the "American Petroleum Co."
   and of the "Caloric"
Sun heat corrugated iron

ADRIENNE LECOUVREUR AND COCTEAU

I have bought two more tiny marmosets
And two birds with feathers like moiré paper
My little monkeys have earrings
My birds have their nails painted gold
I named the smaller monkey Adrienne Lecouvreur and the
   other one Jean
I gave a bird to the daughter of the Argentinian admiral
   who is on board
She is a stupid young girl with a squint in both eyes
She gives her bird a footbath to take the gold off
   its feet
The other one sings in my cabin in a few days he will
   imitate all the familiar sounds and will ring
   like my typewriter
When I write my little monkeys watch me
I am a lot of fun for them
They think they have got me in a cage

HEAT

I am dying from heat in my cabin and I cannot air it
   for fear of exposing my little family of pets to a draught
Too bad
I stay in my cabin
I suffocate and I write I write
I write to please them
These little pets are quite nice and so am I

REQUINS

On m'appelle
Il y a des requins dans notre sillage
Deux trois monstres qui bondissent en virant du blanc
    quand on leur jette des poules
J'achète un mouton que je balance par-dessus bord
Le mouton nage les requins ont peur je suis volé

ENTREPONT

Je passe la soirée dans l'entrepont et dans le poste de
l'équipage
C'est une véritable ménagerie à bord
Bengalis perroquets singes un fourmilier un cachorro do
    matto
De la marmaille nue
Des femmes qui sentent fort

UN TRAIT

Un trait qui s'estompe
Adieu
C'est l'Amérique
Il y a au-dessus une couronne de nuages
Dans la nuit qui vient une étoile de plus belle eau
Maintenant on va cingler vers l'est et à partir de demain
    la piscine sera installée sur le pont supérieur

LE CHARPENTIER

Hic Haec Hoc sont chez le charpentier
Je ne garde dans ma cabine que l'oiseau et les singes
    Adrienne et Cocteau
Chez le charpentier c'est plein de perroquets de singes
    de chiens de chats

SHARKS

Someone is calling me
There are sharks in our wake
Two three monsters which turn white as they breach
    when chickens are thrown to them
I buy a sheep and toss it overboard
The sheep swims the sharks are afraid and I have been had

STEERAGE

I spend the evening in the steerage and the sailors'
    quarters
It is like a real menagerie on board
Bengalese parrots monkeys one anteater a cachorro do
    matto
Naked brats
Ill-smelling women

A LINE

A vanishing line
Farewell
It's America
Above there is a crown of clouds
In the night closing in a star of the most perfect kind
Now we are going to steer toward the east and from
    tomorrow onward the swimming pool will be set up on
    the upper deck

THE CARPENTER

Hic Haec Hoc are with the carpenter
In my cabin I keep only the bird and the monkeys
    Adrienne and Cocteau
The carpenter's room is full of parrots monkeys
    dogs and cats

Lui est un bonhomme qui fume sa pipe
Il a ces yeux gris des buveurs de vin blanc
Quand on parle il vous répond en donnant de grands
   coups de rabot qui font sauter des buchies
En vrille
Je le surnomme Robinson Crusoé
Alors il daigne sourire

JE L'AVAIS BIEN DIT

Je l'avais dit
Quand on achète des singes
Il faut prendre ceux qui sont bien vivants et qui vous
   font presque peur
Et ne jamais choisir un singe doux endormi qui se blottit
   dans vos bras
Car ce sont des singes drogués qui le lendemain sont
   féroces
C'est ce qui vient d'arriver à une jeune fille qui a été
   mordue au nez

CHRISTOPHE COLOMB

Ce que je perds de vue aujourd'hui en me dirigeant vers
   l'est c'est ce que Christophe Colomb découvrait en se
   dirigeant vers l'ouest
C'est dans ces parages qu'il a vu un premier oiseau blanc
   et noir qui l'a fait tomber à genoux et rendre grâces
   à Dieu
Avec tant d'émotion
Et improviser cette prière baudelairienne qui se trouve
   dans son journal de bord
Et où il demande pardon d'avoir menti tous les jours
   à ses compagnons en leur indiquant un faux point
Pour qu'ils ne puissent retrouver sa route

He is a pipe-smoking fellow
He has those grey eyes of white-wine drinkers
When you talk to him he answers with strong pushes
    of his plane which send off splinters
Spinning
I nickname him Robinson Crusoe
Then he grants a smile

DIDN'T I SAY SO!

I said so
When you buy monkeys
You must take those that are very much alive and almost
    frighten you
And never choose a gentle sleepy monkey that nestles
    in your arms
Because they are drugged monkeys which are ferocious
    the next day
That's what happened to a young girl whose nose was bitten

CHRISTOPHER COLUMBUS

As I sail eastward today I am losing sight of what
    Christopher Columbus discovered when sailing westward
It is in these areas that he saw the first black and white bird
    which made him fall to his knees and thank the Lord
With such emotion
And improvise that Baudelairian prayer which is entered in
    his logbook
And where he asks to be forgiven for lying every day to his
    companions indicating to them a false position
So that they may not find his route again

RIRE

Je ris

Je ris
Tu ris
Nous rions
Plus rien ne compte
Sauf ce rire que nous aimons
Il faut savoir être bête et content

LE COMMANDANT EST UN CHIC TYPE

Le commandant est tout de même un chic type
Hier il a fait monter la piscine pour moi seul
Aujourd'hui sans rien dire à personne et tout simplement
   pour me faire plaisir
Il fait un crochet
Et longe Fernando de Noronha de si près que je pourrais
   presque cueillir un bouquet

FERNANDO DE NORONHA

De loin on dirait une cathédrale engloutie
De près
C'est une île aux couleurs si intenses que le vert de
   l'herbe est tout doré

GROTTE

Il y a une grotte qui perce l'île de part en part

LAUGHTER

I laugh

I laugh
You laugh
We laugh
Nothing else matters
But the laughter we love
The point is to know how to be stupid and happy

THE CAPTAIN IS A GOOD GUY

The captain is a good guy all the same
Yesterday he had the pool set up for me alone
Today without a word to anyone and just to please me
He makes a detour
And sails so close to Fernando de Noronha that I can
    almost pick a bunch of flowers

FERNANDO DE NORONHA

From a distance it looks like a submerged cathedral
Seen closer
It is an island with colors so intense that the
    green of the grass is all golden

GROTTO

There is a grotto that bores through the island here and there

PIC

Il y a un pic dont personne n'a pu me dire le nom
Il ressemble au Cervin et c'est le dernier pilier de l'Atlan-
    tide
Quelle émotion quand je crois découvrir à la lunette les
    traces d'une terrasse atlante

PLAGE

Dans une baie
Derrière un promontoire
Une plage de sable jaune et des palmiers de nacre

BAGNE

Un mur blanc
Haut comme celui d'un cimetière
Il porte l'inscription suivante en caractères gigantesques
    que l'on peut très bien déchiffrer à l'œil nu « Logement
    des prises »

CIVILISATION

Il y a quelques traces de cultures
Quelques maisons
Une station de T.S.F. deux pylônes et deux tours Eiffel
    en construction
Un vieux port portugais
Un calvaire
A la lunette je distingue sur le mur du bagne un homme
    nu qui agite un chiffon blanc
Les nuits sont les plus belles sans lune avec des étoiles
    immenses et la chaleur ne va que grandissante
Comme l'agitation des hélices rend l'eau nocturne de
    plus en plus phosphorescente dans notre sillage

PEAK

There is a peak but no one could tell me its name
It looks like the Matterhorn and it is the last pillar
    of Atlantis
What emotion when I think that through the binoculars
    I have discovered evidence of an Atlantean ridge

BEACH

In a bay
Behind a cape
A yellow sand beach and mother-of-pearl palm trees

CONVICT PRISON

A white wall
As high as a graveyard wall
On it the following words appear in huge characters
    very easy to decipher with a naked eye "Prisoners'
    Quarters"

CIVILIZATION

Some traces of cultivated land
A few houses
A radio station two pylons and two Eiffel towers
    under construction
An old Portuguese port
A wayside cross
Through the telescope I can see on the prison wall
    a naked man waving a white cloth
Nights are most beautiful moonless with immense stars
    and the heat keeps intensifying
Just as the propeller's stir makes the nocturnal water in
    our wake gleam more and more luminously

PASSAGERS

Ils sont tous là à faire de la chaise longue
Ou à jouer aux cartes
Ou à prendre le thé
Ou à s'ennuyer
Il y a tout de même un petit groupe de sportifs qui
    jouent aux galets
Ou au deck-tennis
Et un autre petit groupe qui vient nager dans la piscine
La nuit quand tout le monde est couché les fauteuils vides
    alignés sur le pont ressemblent à une collection de
    squelettes dans un musée
Vieilles femmes desséchées
Caméléons pellicules ongles

L'OISEAU BLEU

Mon oiseau bleu a le ventre tout bleu
Sa tête est d'un vert mordoré
Il a une tache noire sous la gorge
Ses ailes sont bleues avec des touffes de petites plumes
    jaune doré
Au bout de la queue il y a des traces de vermillon
Son dos est zébré de noir et de vert
Il a le bec noir les pattes incarnat et deux petits yeux de
    jais
Il adore faire trempette se nourrit de bananes et pousse
    un cri qui ressemble au sifflement d'un tout petit jet
    de vapeur
On le nomme le septicolore

PASSENGERS

They are all there lounging in deck chairs
Or playing cards
Or having tea
Or being bored
There is however a small group of sport lovers
    playing shuffleboard
Or deck tennis
And another small group who come and swim in the pool
At night when everybody is in bed the empty deck chairs
    in a row on the deck look like a collection of
    skeletons in a museum
Old dried-up women
Chameleons dandruff nails

BLUE BIRD

My blue bird's breast is all blue
Its head is bronze green
There is a black spot under its throat
Its wings are blue with tufts of small gold-yellow
    feathers
At the tip of its tail are spots of scarlet
Its back is striped black and green
It has a black beak carnation-red feet and two small
    jet-black eyes
It adores having a dip feeds on bananas and utters a cry
    that sounds like the hiss of a tiny steam jet
It is called the septicolored bird

POURQUOI

L'oiseau siffle
Les singes le regardent
Maîtrise
Je travaille en souriant
Tout ce qui m'arrive m'est absolument égal
Et tout ce que je fais m'est absolument indifférent
Je suis des yeux quelqu'un qui n'est pas là
J'écris en tournant le dos à la marche du navire
Soleil dans le brouillard
Avance
Retard
Oui

OISEAUX

Les rochers guaneux sont remplis d'oiseaux

JANGADA

Trois hommes nus au large
Montés sur une jangada ils chassent au cachalot
Trois poutres blanches une voile triangulaire un balancier

SILLAGE

La mer continue à être d'un bleu de mer
Le temps continue à être le plus beau temps que j'ai
     jamais connu en mer
Cette traversée continue à être la plus calme et la plus
     dépourvue d'incidents que l'on puisse imaginer

WHY

The bird whistles
The monkeys watch it
Self-control
I work with a smile
I could not care less about all that happens to me
And I am totally indifferent to all I do
My eyes follow someone who is not there
I write with my back turned against the ship's course
Sun through the fog
Progress
Delay
Yes

BIRDS

The guano-covered rocks are full of birds

JANGADA

Three naked men in the offing
Sperm whale hunting in a jangada
Three white beams a triangular sail an outrigger

WAKE

The sea remains sea blue
The weather remains the finest I have ever known at sea
This crossing remains the calmest and the most trouble-free
    you can imagine

BAL

Un couple américain danse des danses apaches
Les jeunes Argentines boudent l'orchestre et méprisent
    cordialement les jeunes gens du bord
Les Portugais éclatent en applaudissements dès qu'on
    joue un air portugais
Les Français font bande à part rient fort et se moquent
    de tout le monde
Seules les petites bonnes ont envie de danser dans leurs
    belles robes
J'invite la nourrice nègre au grand scandale des uns et
    pour l'amusement des autres
Le couple américain redanse des danses apaches

PODOMÈTRE

Quand on fait les cent pas sur le pont...

POURQUOI J'ÉCRIS ?

Parce que...

                                                    1924.

DANCING

An American couple dances apache dances
The young Argentinian girls resent the orchestra and
    heartily scorn the young men on board
The Portuguese break into applause as soon as a Portuguese
    tune is played
The French keep to themselves laugh loudly and make fun of
    everyone
Only the young servant girls want to dance in their
    beautiful dresses
Shocking some and diverting others I invite the black nurse
The American couple again dances apache dances

PEDOMETER

When you pace up and down the deck . . .

WHY DO I WRITE?

Because . . .

                                                        1924.

SUD-AMÉRICAINES

SOUTH AMERICAN WOMEN

I

La route monte en lacets
L'auto s'élève brusque et puissante
Nous grimpons dans un tintamarre d'avion qui va pla-
    fonner
Chaque tournant la jette contre mon épaule et quand
    nous virons dans le vide elle se cramponne incons-
    ciente à mon bras et se penche au-dessus du préci-
    pice
Au sommet de la serra nous nous arrêtons court devant
    la faille géante
Une lune monstrueuse et toute proche monte derrière
    nous
« Lua, lua! » murmure-t-elle
Au nom de la lune, mon ami, comment Dieu autorise-t-il
    ces gigantesques travaux qui nous permirent de
    passer?
Ce n'est pas la lune, chérie, mais le soleil qui en préci-
    pitant les brouillards fit cette énorme déchirure
Regarde l'eau qui coule au fond parmi les débris des
    montagnes et qui s'engouffre dans les tuyaux de
    l'usine
Cette station envoie de l'électricité jusqu'à Rio

II

Libertins et libertines
Maintenant nous pouvons avouer
Nous sommes quelques-uns de par le monde
Santé intégrale
Nous avons aussi les plus belles femmes du monde
Simplicité
Intelligence
Amour
Sports
Nous leur avons aussi appris la liberté
Les enfants grandissent avec les chiens les chevaux les
    oiseaux au milieu des belles servantes toutes rondes
    et mobiles comme des tournesols

I

The winding road goes up
The car climbs up rough and powerful
We drive up in the roaring racket of a plane reaching
    its ceiling
Each bend throws her against my shoulder and when we
    take a turn in the void she unconsciously hangs
    onto my arm and leans over the precipice
At the top of the ridge we stop short in front of a
    gigantic fault
An enormous moon rises very close behind us
"Lua, lua!" she whispers
In the name of the moon, my friend, why does God permit
    these huge constructions that enable us to
    get through?
Not the moon, darling, but the sun precipitating the fogs
    made this huge rift
Look at the water running at the bottom through the
    mountain's rubble and rushing into the factory's pipes
This station provides electricity as far as Rio

II

Libertines, men and women*
Now we can confess
There are a few of us throughout the world
Perfect health
We also have the most beautiful wives in the world
Simplicity
Intelligence
Love
Sports
We also taught them freedom
Children grow up with dogs horses birds among beautiful
    servant girls all round and mobile like sunflowers

III

Il n'y a plus de jalousie de crainte ou de timidité
Nos amies sont fortes et saines
Elles sont belles et simples et grandes
Et elles savent toutes s'habiller
Ce ne sont pas des femmes intelligentes mais elles sont
   très perspicaces
Elles n'ont pas peur d'aimer
Elles ne craignent pas de prendre
Elles savent tout aussi bien donner
Chacune d'elles a dû lutter avec sa famille leur position
   sociale le monde ou autre chose
Maintenant
Elles ont simplifié leur vie et sont pleines d'enfantillages
Plus de meubles plus de bibelots elles aiment les animaux
   les grandes automobiles et leur sourire
Elles voyagent
Elles détestent la musique mais emportent toutes un
   phono

IV

Il y en a trois que j'aime particulièrement
La première
Une vieille dame sensible belle et bonne
Adorablement bavarde et d'une souveraine élégance
Mondaine mais d'une gourmandise telle qu'elle s'est
   libérée de la mondanité
La deuxième est la sauvageonne de l'Hôtel Meurice
Tout le jour elle peigne ses longs cheveux et grignote
   son rouge de chez Guerlain
Bananiers nourrice nègre colibris
Son pays est si loin qu'on voyage six semaines sur un
   fleuve recouvert de fleurs de mousses de champignons
   gros comme des œufs d'autruche
Elle est si belle le soir dans le hall de l'hôtel que tous les
   hommes en sont fous
Son sourire le plus aigu est pour moi car je sais rire comme
   les abeilles sauvages de son pays

III

No more jealousy fear shyness
Our girl friends are strong and healthy
They are beautiful simple and tall
And all know how to dress
They are not intelligent women but they are very
    perceptive
They are not afraid to love
They take without fear
They know just as well how to give
Each of them has had to struggle against her family
    her social position the world or something else
Now
They have simplified their life and are full of nonsense
No more furniture no more trinkets they love animals
    big cars and their smile
They travel
They detest music but all carry along a record player

IV

There are three of them I particularly like
The first
An old lady sensitive beautiful and kind
Delightfully talkative and with a regal elegance
A society woman but so greedy that she liberated herself
    from social life
The second is the wild one from the Hotel Meurice
All day long she combs her hair and nibbles at her
    Guerlain lipstick
Banana trees black wet nurse hummingbird
Her country is so far away that you travel six weeks on a river
    covered with flowers moss mushrooms as large as
    ostrich eggs
She is so beautiful in the evening in the hotel lobby that
    all the men are crazy about her
Her sharpest smile is for me because I know how to laugh
    like the wild bees in her country

La dernière est trop riche pour être heureuse
Mais elle a déjà fait de grands progrès
Ce n'est pas du premier coup que l'on trouve son équilibre
    et la simplicité de la vie au milieu de toutes les compli-
    cations de la richesse
Il y faut de l'entêtement
Elle le sait bien elle qui monte si divinement à cheval et
    qui fait corps avec son grand étalon argentin
Que ta volonté soit comme ta cravache
Mais ne t'en sers pas
Trop
Souvent

V

Il y en a encore une autre qui est encore comme une toute
    petite fille
Malgré son horrible mari ce divorce affreux et la déten-
    tion au cloître
Elle est farouche comme le jour et la nuit
Elle est plus belle qu'un œuf
Plus belle qu'un rond
Mais elle est toujours trop nue sa beauté déborde elle ne
    sait pas encore s'habiller
Elle mange aussi beaucoup trop et son ventre s'arrondit
    comme si elle était enceinte de deux petits mois
C'est qu'elle a un tel appétit et une telle envie de vivre
Nous allons lui apprendre tout ça et lui apprendre à
    s'habiller
Et lui donner les bonnes adresses

VI

Une
Il y en a encore une
Une que j'aime plus que tout au monde
Je me donne à elle tout entier comme une pepsine car
    elle a besoin d'un fortifiant
Car elle est trop douce

The last one is too rich to be happy
But she has already improved a lot
You can't find all at once your balance and the simplicity
    of life amid all the complexities of wealth
You need obstinacy
She knows it well she who rides so divinely and is all
    one with her tall Argentinian stallion
Let your will be like your crop
But don't use it
Too
Often

V

There is still another one who remains a very little girl
In spite of her awful husband this hideous divorce and
    detention in a convent
She is withdrawn like day and night
She is more beautiful than an egg
More beautiful than a circle
But she is always too naked her beauty spills over
    she does not yet know how to dress
She also eats much too much and her stomach bulges
    as if she were two little months pregnant
Actually she has such an appetite and such craving
    for life
We'll teach her all that and teach her how to dress
And give her the good addresses to know

VI

One
There is still one more
One whom I love more than anything in the world
I give my whole self to her like pepsin for she
    needs a tonic
For she is too gentle

Car elle est encore un peu craintive
Car le bonheur est une chose bien lourde à porter
Car la beauté a besoin d'un petit quart d'heure d'exercice
    tous les matins

VII

Nous ne voulons pas être tristes
C'est trop facile
C'est trop bête
C'est trop commode
On en a trop souvent l'occasion
C'est pas malin
Tout le monde est triste
Nous ne voulons plus être tristes

1924.

For she is still a little fearful
For happiness is a very heavy load to bear
For beauty needs a daily dozen every morning

VII

We refuse to be sad
It's too easy
It's too stupid
It's too convenient
We are given the chance too often
It's not smart
Everybody is sad
We refuse to be sad any longer

1924.

Notes on the Poems

WEST (p. 49). It is obvious from the context of the poems included under this title that Cendrars was referring to the East Coast. He probably used the title "*WEST*" (in English in the original French text) facetiously to stress that the East Coast of North America is west to a Parisian.

Dawn tarries / That (p. 55). In this typically Cendrarian elliptical construction the syntactical conventions are broken to achieve a more stunning effect of speed and efficiency, together with a touch of irony. I have tried to preserve the effect in English insofar as possible in spite of the apparently illogical use of "that."

Jackrabbit (p. 61). The humor in the fanciful juxtaposition of the American names of the animals mentioned is lost in translation. We may assume that Cendrars did mean jackrabbit since in the other two instances he gave the proper equivalent to the French.

cures her pig's skin (p. 67). Cendrars effectively coins a verb out of the French substantive *couenne* which means the thick skin of a pig or the rind of bacon. The English allows only an approximate transposition.

makeshift sails (p. 67). The phrase *voiles de fortune* may also mean foresails or crossjacks. Cendrars undoubtedly meant to play on the double meaning of the expression.

ptarmigans (p. 87). As in the poem "Cucumingo," the humorous exoticism of the local American name inserted into the French text is lost in translation. *Perdrix de neige* are ptarmigans.

La Pallice (p. 127). La Pallice is an outer port of La Rochelle on the Atlantic coast of France in Charente-Maritime. In the last line Cendrars plays with the homonym M. de la Palice, although he keeps the spelling of the harbor name. Jacques de Chabannes de la Palice (1470-1525) was a French marshal who died at Pavie. Upon his death his soldiers composed a song,

> A quarter of an hour before he died
> He was still alive . . .,

implying that he fought to the last minute. Gradually, however, the naive truism of these words became a sample of what the French call a *vérité de la Palice* (truth of M. de la Palice) or *lapalissade*.

Salon d'Automne (p. 141). The *Salon d'Automne,* a famous avant-garde painting exhibit which opened in Paris in 1903, presented the first cubist painters—Braque, Picasso, Picabia—as well as Soutine and the "simultaneous" paintings of Robert Delaunay. It started a notorious battle when a member of the Chamber of Deputies, who requested the removal of some of the works at the salon, was told that no law could control the exhibits or order the artists what to paint but that he could always order his eyes not to look at them.

Equatoria (p. 153). This is the only title mentioned in the poem which does not refer to a work that Cendrars had already published or would publish later. *Moravagine* was published by Grasset in 1926. *Le Plan de l'aiguille* was published by Sans Pareil in 1929. Cendrars did write *La création du Monde* for the Swedish Ballet which was first performed in October 1923 with the music of Darius Milhaud, choreography by Jean Borlin, and stage scenery and costumes designed by Fernand Léger. Although there is an unpublished record of a ballet libretto entitled *Après-diner*, there is no evidence that it was done for Erik Satie. "Coeur du Monde" refers to a poem Cendrars had written in 1917. Only a fragment had been published in *Littérature* in August 1919, but the poem was included in *Poésies Complètes* (1944). The *Anthologie* refers to the *L'Anthologie nègre*, the first volume of which appeared in 1921. In 1928 Cendrars brought out *Petits Contes Nègres pour les enfants des Blancs*.

The Pitch Pole (p. 159). This poem is a typical translator's trap. Cendrars builds the whole structure of his text on the homophony of *pot au noir* (the real phrase in French for pitch pot) and *poteau noir* (black pole). The more common term for *pot au noir* in America is "doldrums." In order to stay as close as possible to Cendrars's puns, however, I chose the old British sailor's term "pitch pot."

Jean ... Erik ... Fernand (p. 171). The names mentioned in this poem are not haphazard inventions by Cendrars. They are all the first names of friends in artistic and literary circles: Jean Cocteau; Erik Satie; Fernand Léger; Eugenia Errazuris, a well-known patron of artists; Marcel Lévesque, a well-known actor who was Cendrars's neighbor in Le Tremblay; Mariette Prado, wife of Paul Prado, a South American man of letters and businessman who invited Cendrars to São Paulo; Francis Picabia; Germaine Everling, an intimate friend of Picabia's; Abel Gance, a film director with whom Cendrars cooperated on the film *La roue*; and Raymone, an actress, the poet's lifelong friend whom he married in 1949.

Coalsack (p. 207). Cendrars mentions the Coalsack again in *Le Lotissement du ciel* (Denoël, (1949), where in his imaginative manner he explains the source and the meaning of the phrase:

> ... it is the abyss that in Brazil the natives call the *Coalsack* [italics in the original], as if to say "the entrance to hell, the cave of the Devourer of the World,"
> In these latitudes the Southern Cross is master of the hemi-

sphere. The *Coalsack* is exactly situated below and slightly to the left of the theoretical meeting point of the two branches that form a cross in this symbolic southern constellation. Indeed, you can see there a black pocket, and the more you contemplate it, the deeper it seems. . . .

The *Coalsack* does not appear on any map of the sky. I asked lots of people in Brazil about it. People living inland gave me its exact position and pointed out to me, arm and forefinger outstretched, its slipstream, its folds, and its dark eddies, interpreted its blackness as fortune-tellers interpret inkspots, spoke to me about their local superstitions, crossing themselves many times. . . .

The coast dwellers, the city people and those from the capital had all heard of the *Coalsack*, but could not quite locate it. They discussed endlessly the reality of the phenomenon. . . .

. . . when you ask [the children] about the *Coalsack*, which is not the entrance to hell but, for them, the exit from the world, the opening to the world of wonder, the world of the fairy tales told by their nannies, white, crossbred, or black: *Once upon a time an ogre* . . . [italics in original].

. . . c'est le gouffre que le peuple, au Brésil, appelle le *sac à charbon*, autant dire: l'entrée de l'Enfer, l'antre du Mangeur du Monde.

Sous ces latitudes, la Croix du Sud est maîtresse de l'hémisphère. Le *sac à charbon*, se situe exactement au-dessous et légèrement à gauche du point de rencontre théorique des deux branches en croix de la symbolique constellation sud. En effet, il y a là une poche noire. Et plus on la contemple, plus elle semble profonde [*Le Lotissement du ciel*, Vol. XII of *Oeuvres complètes* (Paris: Club Français du Livre, 1970), pp. 192-193].

Le "*sac à charbon*" ne figure sur aucune carte céleste. J'ai interrogé des tas de gens au Brésil. Les gens de l'intérieur le situaient exactement et me le désignaient le bras, l'index tendus, me faisaient suivre son sillage, ses plis, ses remous sombres, interprétaient sa noirceur comme les diseuses de bonne aventure interprètent les taches d'encre, me parlaient de leurs superstitions paysannes en faisant de nombreux signes de croix. . . .

Les gens du littoral, des grandes villes et de la capitale avaient entendu parler du "*sac à charbon*," le situaient mal et discutaient à l'infini de la réalité du phénomène. . . .

. . . quand on les [les enfants] interroge sur le "*sac à charbon*," qui n'est l'entrée de l'Enfer, mais, pour eux, la sortie du Monde, la bouche du merveilleux, le monde des contes de leur nounou, blanche, métissée ou négresse: *Il y avait une fois un ogre* . . . [*Ibid*, pp. 193, 194, 195].

Libertines P. 235). This poem might be considered as Cendrars's final dismissal of an old cherished project of writing a book he planned to entitle "Les Libertins," for which he did extensive research in the library of Saint Petersburg in September 1911 and the Bibliothèque Nationale in Paris in October 1912.

BIBLIOGRAPHY

WORKS OF BLAISE CENDRARS

Only first editions are listed here, in order of publication. For a complete bibliography of publications in reviews and magazines, translations, and reprints consult Volume XV of the Club Français du Livre edition of *Oeuvres complètes*.

1909: *Novgorod, le légende de l'or gris et du silence*. Moscow: Sozonoff.

1912: *Les Pâques*. Paris: Édition des Hommes Nouveaux.

1913: *La Prose du Transsibérien et de la Petite Jeanne de France*. Paris: Édition des Hommes Nouveaux.
Séquences. Paris: Édition des Hommes Nouveaux.

1916: *La Guerre au Luxembourg*. Paris: Niestlé.

1917: *Profond Aujourd'hui*. Paris: À la Belle Édition.

1918: *Le Panama ou les Aventures de mes sept oncles*. Paris: Éditions de la Sirène..
J'ai tué. Paris: À la Belle Édition.

1919: *Du Monde Entier (Les Pâques à New York; Prose du Transsibérien; Panama)* Paris: Éditions de la Nouvelle Revue Française.
Dix-neuf poèmes élastiques. Paris: Au Sans Pareil.
La fin du monde filmée par l'ange Notre-Dame. Paris: Éditions de la Sirène.

1921: *L'Anthologie nègre*. Paris: Éditions de la Sirène.

1922: *La perle fiévreuse*. In *Signaux de France et de Belgique*, nos. 7, 9, 10, 11-12.
Moganni Nameh. in *Les Feuilles Libres*, nos. 25, 26, 27, 28, 29, 30.

1924: *Kodak (Documentaires)*. Paris: Stock, Dellamain, Boutelleau.
Le Formose. Part I of *Feuilles de route*. Paris: Au Sans Pareil.

1925: *L'Or*. Paris: Grasset.

1926: *Moravagine*. Paris: Grasset.
L'Eubage: Aux antipodes de l'Unité. Paris: Au Sans Pareil.
L'A B C du cinéma. Paris: Les Écrivains Réunis.

1928: *Petits Contes nègres pour les enfants des Blancs*. Paris: Les Éditions du Portique.

1929: *Le Plan de l'aiguille*. Paris: Au Sans Pareil.
      Les Confessions de Dan Yack. Paris: Au Sans Pareil.
      Une Nuit dans la forêt. Paris: Les Éditions du Verseau.
1930: *Rhum: L'aventure de Jean Galmot*. Paris: Grasset.
      Comment les Blancs sont d'anciens Noirs. Paris: Au Sans Pareil.
1931: *Aujourd'hui*. Paris: Grasset.
1932: *Vol à Voile*. Lausanne: Payot.
1935: *Panorama de la pègre*. Grenoble: Arthaud.
1936: *Hollywood: La Mecque du cinéma*. Paris: Grasset.
1937: *Histoires vraies*. Paris: Grasset.
1938: *La vie dangereuse*. Paris: Grasset.
1940: *D'Oultremer à indigo*. Paris: Grasset.
      Chez l'armée anglaise. Paris: Éditions Corrêa.
1944: *Poésies complètes de Blaise Cendrars*. With introduction by Jacques-Henry Lévesque. Paris: Denoël.
1945: *L'Homme foudroyé*. Paris: Denoël.
1946: *La Main coupée*. Paris: Denoël.
1948: *Bourlinguer*. Paris: Denoël.
1949: *Le Lotissement du ciel*. Paris: Denoël.
      La banlieue de Paris. Lausanne: La Guilde du Livre; Paris: Éditions Pierre Seghers.
1952: *Blaise Cendrars vous parle*. Paris: Denoël.
      Le Brésil, des hommes sont venus. Monaco: Les Documents d'Art.
1953: *Noël aux quatre coins du monde*. Paris: Denoël.
1956: *Entretien de Fernand Léger avec Blaise Cendrars et Louis Carré sur le paysage dans l'oeuvre de Léger*. Paris: Louis Carré.
      Emmène-moi au bout du monde. Paris: Denoël.
1957: *Trop c'est trop*. Paris: Denoël.
1958: *A l'Aventure* (selections from earlier works). Paris: Denoël.
1959: *Films sans images*. In collaboration with Nino Frank. Paris: Denoël.
1960-1965: *Oeuvres complètes de Blaise Cendrars*. 8 vols. Paris: Denoël.
1969: *Blaise Cendrars: Inédits Secrets*. Presented by Myriam Cendrars. Paris: Club Français du Livre.
1968-1971: *Oeuvres complètes de Blaise Cendrars*. 15 vols. Included, in addition to all previously published works: *John Paul Jones* (1926), in Vol. XIV; *Les rêves perdus de Blaise Cendrars* (1951), in Vol. XIII; text of television broadcast on Modigliani (1955), in Vol. XIII. Paris: Club Français du Livre).

WORKS OF BLAISE CENDRARS TRANSLATED INTO ENGLISH

1919: *I have Killed (J'ai tué). The Plowshare* (Woodstock, N.Y.), no. 6/7.
1922: *Profound To-day (Profond Aujourd'hui). Broom: International
       Magazine of the Arts* (London, Rome, Zurich), I, no. 3 (January).
       At the Antipodes of Unity (L'Eubage). Ibid., III, no. 3 (October).
1926: *Sutter's Gold (L'Or).* New York: Harper (repr. 1936, 1954);
       London: Heinemann.
1927: *African Saga (Anthologie nègre).* New York: Boards Payson &
       Clark.
1929: *Little Black Stories for Little White Children (Petits Contes
       nègres pour les enfants des Blancs).* New York: Harcourt
       Brace.
1930: *Sutter's Gold.* First edition in Braille. Los Angeles.
1931: *Panama (The Prose of the Transsiberian; Panama;* excerpts from
       Kodak and from Part I of *Feuilles de route).* Translated, intro-
       duced, and illustrated by John Dos Passos. New York: Harper.
       John Paul Jones. In *The European Caravan.* Ed. Samuel Putnam.
       New York: Brewer, Warren and Putnam.
       I Have No Regrets (from Cendrars's translation of *Feu le lieu-
       tenant Bringolf).* Trans. Warre B. Wells. Ed. Blaise Cendrars.
       London: Jarrolds.
1948: *Antarctic Fugue (Le Plan de l'aiguille)* London: Pushkin Press;
       New York: Anglobooks.
1962: *Selected Writings* (complete earlier poems; two poems from
       Documentaires; five poems from *Feuilles de route;* selections
       from prose works). Edited with introduction by Walter Albert.
       Preface by Henry Miller. New York: New Directions (repr.
       1966).
1966: *To the End of the World (Emmène-moi au bout du monde).*
       London: Peter Owen; New York: Grove Press, 1968.
       Excerpts from *Blaise Cendrars vous parle* and *L'Homme fou-
       droyé* and eleven poems from *Du Monde entier au coeur du
       Monde.* Introduction by William Brandon. *Paris Review,* X,
       no. 37.
1968: *Moravagine.* London: Peter Owen: New York: Doubleday, 1970.
       "Two Portraits: Gustave Lerouge and Arthur Cravan." *Paris
       Review,* XI, no. 42.
1970: *The Astonished Man (L'Homme foudroyé).* London: Peter Owen.
1972: *Planus (Bourlinguer).* London: Peter Owen.
1973: *Lice (La Main coupée).* London: Peter Owen.

SELECTED WORKS ON CENDRARS

Reviews of Blaise Cendrars's works and articles on him have appeared in practically all major newspapers and literary reviews in France, England, Germany, Italy, and the United States. Numerous unpublished theses have been written in England, France, and the United States. The following list is limited to books and chapters in books on Cendrars, but it also includes two special issues of literary reviews devoted entirely to Cendrars.

Albert, Walter. Introduction to *Selected Writings of Blaise Cendrars.* New York: New Directions, 1962, 1966.

Amaral, Aracy A. *Blaise Cendrars no Brasil e os modernistos.* São Paulo: Martins Press, 1970.

Bozon Scalziti, Yvette. *Blaise Cendrars et le symbolisme, de Moganni Nameh au Transsibérien.* Archives des Lettres modernes. Paris: Minard, 1972.

Buhler, Jean. *Blaise Cendrars, homme libre, poète au coeur du monde.* Bienne, Switzerland: Éditions du Panorama, 1960.

Caws, Mary Ann. "Blaise Cendrars: A Cinema of Poetry." In *The Inner Theatre of Recent French Poetry.* Princeton: Princeton University Press, 1972.

Chadourne, Jacqueline. *Blaise Cendrars, poète du Cosmos.* Paris: Seghers, 1973.

Lepage, Albert. *Blaise Cendrars: étude critique.* Paris: Les Écrivains Réunis, 1926.

Lévesque, Jacques-Henry. *Blaise Cendrars ou Du Monde entier au coeur du Monde: Introduction aux poésies complètes de Blaise Cendrars,* Paris: Denoël, 1944.

———. *Blaise Cendrars: Étude suivie d'une anthologie des plus belles pages.* Paris: Éditions de la Nouvelle Revue Critique, 1947.

Lovey, Jean-Claude. *Situation de Blaise Cendrars.* Neuchâtel: À la Baconnière, 1965.

Mercure de France. No. 1185 (May 1962). *Blaise Cendrars.*

Miller, Henry. "Tribute to Blaise Cendrars." *T'ien Hsia* (Shanghai), vol. 7 (1938). Repr. in *The Wisdom of the Heart.* New York: New Directions, 1941. Pp. 151-158.

———. "Blaise Cendrars." In *Books in My Life.* New York: New Directions, 1952. Pp. 58-80.

———. *Blaise Cendrars.* Translation of above articles by François Villié. Paris: Denoël, 1951.

Parrot, Louis, *Blaise Cendrars.* With bibliography by Jacques-Henry Lévesque. Poètes d'aujourd'hui. Paris: Seghers, 1948.

Poupon, Marc. *Guillaume Apollinaire et Cendrars*. Archives des Lettres Modernes, no. 103. Paris: Minard, 1969.

Richard, Hugues. *Dites-nous Monsieur Blaise Cendrars*. Lausanne: Éditions Rencontres, 1969.

Risques. Special issue, no. 9-10 (1954). *Salut, Blaise Cendrars*.

Rousselot, Jean, *Blaise Cendrars*. Collection Témoins du XXE siècle. Paris: Éditions Universitaires, 1955.

T'serstevens, A. *L'homme que fut Blaise Cendrars*. Paris: Denoël, 1972.

BIBLIOGRAPHICAL NOTE ON *Ocean Letters* (*Feuilles de route*)

The three parts of *Feuilles de route* were not grouped together in one volume until Denoël published *Poésies complètes* in 1944. They were first published separately as follows:

Part I: *Le Formose*. Paris: Au Sans Pareil, 1924. 78 pp.

Part II: *São-Paulo*. In Catalogue of the Tarsila Exhibit. Paris: Percier Gallery, 1926. The same year the gallery issued a special brochure containing the six poems.

Part III: "Départ" through "Un jour viendra." *Montparnasse*, no. 49 (February-March 1927). "Coucher de soleil" through "Pourquoi j'écris?" *Montparnasse*, no. 51 (May-June 1928).

It is of interest to note that in the first edition of *Feuilles de Route* (Paris: Au Sans Pareil, 1924) Cendrars announced five parts to this collection, as follows: Part I, Le Formose; Part II, Sao Paulo; Part III, Rio de Janeiro; Part IV, A la Fazenda; Part V, Des hommes sont venus. In 1952 the title of Part V became the subtitle of his book on Brazil (see Bibliography).